# COLOURSCAPE

# COLOURSCAPE

## MICHAEL LANCASTER

ACADEMY EDITIONS

To Renate, who helps me to see.

*ACKNOWLEDGEMENTS*
I wish to thank my former colleagues in the University of Greenwich — Patrick Goode, Carol Jones, Tom Turner, Heather Blackett and Roger Seijo — for continuing to draw my attention to colour issues. In addition I should like to thank those who have responded to particular enquiries, including Panos Arvantatakis, Simon Bell, Geoffrey Broadbent, Thom Gorst, Elisabeth Gruenagel, Richard Harris, Malcolm Haxby, Carol Jones, Georgina Livingston, Hannah McCluskey, Jane McDermott, Alec Nash, Anthony Quiney, Clarissa Rosenow, Viren Sahai, Nicholas Shepherd and Harry Teggin, although the views expressed are my own. Also, thanks to Julia Weiss for some translation from Russian.

I am grateful to Derek Abbott for his comments on the subjects of planning and conservation, to Robert Travers for comments on the biological material and to Roy Osborne and Nick Pillans for comments on the earlier chapters concerned with perception; also to Jeremy Greenwood of Quiller Press for permission to use material from my previous book *Britain in View: Colour and the Landscape*, 1984, to V&K Publishing (Laren, The Netherlands), for permission to use material published in *The Colour of the City*, 1992, and to the individuals and organisations who have assisted in the promotion of various colour studies, including: the Civic Trust, the North Devon District Council, the London Borough of Greenwich, Central Television, the Sikkens Foundation and AKZO Nobel. In particular, I acknowledge a long-standing debt to Jean-Philippe Lenclos for demonstrating to me the essential connection between colour and the environment.

I wish to thank Rachel Beckett and the staff of Academy Editions for their patience and help.

*PHOTOGRAPHIC CREDITS*
The author wishes to thank the following individuals and organisations who supplied illustrations: the Architectural Association/Andrew Higgott, p40; the Architectural Association/Petra Hodgson, p107; the Architectural Association/Taylor Galyean, p109 (below); AEA Technology/Andrew Rees, cover, p14 (above left); Colin Baxter Photography Ltd, p21; Simon Bell (Forestry Commission), p87; Heather Blackett, p63; Edward Butcher, p14 (above right); Giancarlo de Carlo, pp28, 29; Crown Copyright, by permission of HMSO, p38; Farmer & Dark, p14 (right, above and centre); Faulks, Perry, Culley & Rech, p14 (below right); Roy Furness, pp24, 62 (below left); AC Hughes, p76; Carol Jones, p77; Chris Guy, p112; Jean-Philippe Lenclos for the wealth of material he has supplied to illustrate his method and several examples of colour design, pp68-71; Jean-Philippe Lenclos/René Robert, p71 (above right); Nicholas Pearson & Partners and Sillson Photography, Wareham, p14 (left, centre and below), back cover; Viren Sahai, pp 69, 71; British Library, p12 (above); Speirs & Major, p114; Tagliasacchi & Zanetta, pp82, 83, 84, 85; Tate Gallery, London, p60; Tom Turner, p55 (below). The remaining photographs are by the author. Attempts have been made to locate the sources of all photographs to obtain full production rights, but in the very few cases where this process has failed to find the copyright holder, apologies are offered.

*FRONT COVER: Detail of Winfrith Technology Centre, Dorset (colour design: Nicholas Pearson Associates); BACK COVER: General view of Winfrith*

*FRONTISPIECE: View from Can Cayrou, near Calmeilles, Roussillon, Pyrenees.*
*The blue of the sky and the layers of blue haze covering distant mountains are an effect of the scattering of the short blue wavelengths of light caused by particles of moisture and dust between the viewer and the object*

First published in 1996 by
ACADEMY EDITIONS,
an imprint of

ACADEMY GROUP LTD
42 Leinster Gardens, London W2 3AN
Member of the VCH Publishing Group

ISBN 1 85490 451 5

Distributed to the trade in the United States of America by
NATIONAL BOOK NETWORK, INC
4720 Boston Way, Lanham, Maryland 20706

Printed and bound in Singapore

# CONTENTS

# PREFACE

This book is about colour and architecture: but it is not particularly about outstanding buildings, which are well covered elsewhere. More specifically it is about colours themselves, their relationship to one another and their relationship to their surroundings — for no colour is ever seen in isolation. The views of the buildings and objects that I have selected are not necessarily the best views — although that is always a temptation — because I wish to show them in context. I have, moreover, tried to avoid the pitfalls of the static view based upon the principle of fixed-point perspective, attempting instead to come to terms with the essential mobility of our perceptions. Also, I have tried to avoid the jargon of architecture (although I must confess to an exception in the title), since the subject of colour is already too heavily encumbered with its own scientific language.

In writing my previous book on the subject of colour I soon became aware of significant discrepancies of perception by writers and practitioners concerned with different aspects of what is, after all, the same subject. While there are many books on colour in painting, there are relatively few on colour and architecture and still fewer on colour in the architectural contexts of townscape and landscape, subject areas of which writers seem wary. Rather than attempting another survey of different aspects of environmental colour, I have tried in the current book to deal with some of the problems arising from a subject that is admittedly extremely complicated. The first limitation is to concern myself principally with buildings; but buildings are not seen in isolation: every one has a context, whether it be in town or country. Since colour depends upon relationships, the context assumes visual importance equal to that of the building itself. .

If we think of buildings as conceived and designed from within, their form and detail echoing their function, colour design is the opposite, working from outside over the buildings and their context. 'Landscape' has become too specialised a word to express this conception of colour, and 'townscape' is too restricted by the uses to which it has been put. The word 'environment' is a poor substitute, with its connotations of ecology, pollution and public health, which have obscured its original French meaning ('surroundings'). Both 'landscape' and 'townscape' have the advantage of being associated with space and with buildings seen from the outside, either as landmarks within the space or enclosing it. Accordingly, I have chosen 'Colourscape' as an appropriate title. (It has the additional advantage of having been used to describe a 'colour experience' comprising plastic tunnels of different colours, designed by Peter Jones and Maurice Agis.)[1]

Books on colour tend to fall into several categories. Those that do not belong to the fairly well-defined artistic, scientific or architectural groups fall rather loosely into categories embracing animals, man and the environment, travel and the countryside, largely in terms of photography. I have attempted — perhaps rashly — to bridge these categories in addressing people in general rather than just specialists. People are now much more aware of architecture than hitherto, if only because of the failures, and everyone is aware of the environment. Moreover, we all experience colour: we use it and have to live with its effects, even if we do not understand what they are. My aim is to simplify and clarify the subject of colour and the ways in which it affects our environment.

MICHAEL LANCASTER, 1996

# INTRODUCTION

We are confused by colour. Just as we begin to come to terms with the scientific explanation of what it is and how and why it occurs, the same questions arise over its perception and then again over its use. It is not surprising that the subject has been treated differently by specialists in every branch of its application. The art historian John Gage writes:

> the way in which the societies of Europe and the United States have shaped and developed their experience of colour falls between too many academic stools. Colour is almost everybody's business but it has rarely been treated in a unified way . . . . failure to look at colour comprehensively has led to absurdities of theory, if not of practice.[2]

As evidence of the failure of theory he cites a number of examples from art; for evidence of the failure of practice, we need only to look around us. But therein lies a problem, for although we may look, we may well not *see*. Common sense tells us that perception is selective: we see what we want to see; we notice things according to our different interests. The brain could not possibly absorb all the information with which our senses are confronted at any one time; information is selected according to its relevance, the remainder being dismissed as redundant. This would provide an explanation for the fact that so much of what might be regarded as visual pollution — in the form of industrial dereliction, massed advertisement hoardings and simply litter — often goes unnoticed. As colour is usually seen only as a property of objects and colour vision is only one aspect of our visual capabilities (being most effective at the close range in which sharp-focus vision occurs), it follows that much colour information is likely to be filtered out. This has a profound bearing on what we might term 'visual illiteracy'.

In nature, colours and the visual systems for perceiving them have evolved in very specialised ways. The functions of colour are to attract attention, to impart information, to aid deception and to stimulate the emotions. Colour vision enables us to see and judge the ripeness of fruits and the freshness of meat, the attractions of a mate and the threat of an enemy. Although in humans this natural faculty remains remarkably strong, it has been blunted by the miscellany of other uses that have been found for colour. Some of these are justified and even logical — for example, its use for signs and symbols — but many are irrelevant.

The sense of personal involvement is most directly concerned with the home, where learning begins: it is there that the miracle of colour is first discovered. This occurs during the first five years of life, after which colours are more generally regarded as aspects of objects or materials. In pre-industrial societies, which we may regard as relatively 'natural', the number of colours seen both inside and outside the home was extremely limited. How, we may ask, can a child cope with the profusion of uncoordinated colour in toys, books, pictures, clothing, furnishings, furniture, carpets and walls? Tests using animals in laboratories suggest that such sensory confusion leads to stress, but human beings are different. It seems likely that we are able to 'switch off', and at some point we learn to distinguish meaningful colours from those that are meaningless.

Although we retain acute perception in matters relating to food and health, we have no option but to accept what we must regard as a biological degeneration of some of our sensory responses, including those concerned with colour vision. However, we can be heartened by the possibilities of learning. Just as design has flourished as a discipline of great diversity to fill the gap left by the decline of the crafts, so it is possible to learn to 'see' colour. While most people have developed restricted habits of seeing, it is significant that many artists have experienced the discovery of colour as a kind of enlightenment. The art theorist John Ruskin referred to 'the innocent eye' of the painter JMW Turner, and the term was later used in reference to the Impressionists. Paul Klee was already thirty-four when his work was transformed by a visit to the Tunisian town Hammamet with August Macke in 1914: 'I have discovered colour', he wrote. He began to see colour in terms of 'the synthesis of urban architecture and pictorial architecture', represented by Paul Cézanne's idea of colour 'as the place where our spirit and the universe meet'.[3] The art historian Will Grohmann noted,

> In the Tunisian watercolours for the first time colour fastens object and space without the aid of line and, as in Cézanne, the ground does not appear between the coloured areas. The modulation of contrasting colours is pushed to the extreme limit, giving rise to rhythmic movement in the direction of the plane as well as vibrations, that is space and time, the assimilation of dream and reality.[4]

FROM ABOVE: 'Colour pollution': The effect of white on this headland at Port Bou, Spain, is apparent for some distance; The comparative visual impact of whitewashed and unpainted stone cottages, North Wales; White has been wrongly used on a new housing settlement on the estuary below Harlech Castle, North Wales, making it too eye-catching

ABOVE: 'Colour pollution': although reds and greens are basically harmonious opposites, their potential for harmony is disrupted here by the diversity of surfaces of different textures, shapes, alignments and character

The present book begins in the chapter entitled The Purpose of Colour by examining origins of colour and colour vision in nature and their relevance to human beings. In From Evolution to Revolution, the author considers briefly the ways in which the uses of colour have been adapted from painting and symbolism to the industrial uses of today. The Nature of Colour is concerned with light and colour as physical phenomena and how colour is affected by different surfaces and distance. The problems of seeing and perception are explored in Colour Perception; this is followed in the chapter entitled In Search of Harmony by a brief investigation of colour classification systems and the most commonly accepted ideas of colour harmony. In Impressions and Expressions the author considers how the exploration into the portrayal of light through colour by such painters as Turner and Monet led to the self-conscious expression of colour in architecture. Colour Effects examines the notional and immeasurable factors influencing our colour perceptions. Colour and Space is an investigation into spatial aspects of colour; the following chapter deals with the related issue of Colour and Place in the light of the large body of material relating to traditional and modern uses of colour. The chapters on Colour Control, Colour Planning and Colour Strategies deal with the use and control of colour in the environment. In Colour Choices the author addresses some of the issues of colour design more directly, and in High Colour the use of colour on high-rise buildings — a problem of the present — is investigated; in Future Colour the implications of colour for future development are considered. With such a subject it is neither possible not desirable to be prescriptive, but guidelines are essential and these have been included as an appendix.

Everyone is interested in colour, and the subject can arouse strong feelings, as can be judged by the reports on the concern of the residents of Bath about the colours of their front doors, described in Colour Control. Similar passions have been aroused by threats to lamp-posts and pillar boxes. The painter Adrian Stokes notes:

. . . how long I had waited to see our glaring pillar boxes given by the light and season a structural relationship in the English countryside! For years they had stood out in my eyes, glaring irrelevantly. On this overcast May day, however, the young leaf-greens of intense luminosity and of the right area and disposition, had come to the rescue, had entered into companionship with the red, and with each other.[5]

# THE PURPOSE OF COLOUR

Tempting as it is to think of colour vision as having been given to us for the purpose of enjoying rainbows and sunsets, the reality is at once more mundane and more remarkable. The phenomenon of colour vision, which humans share in various ways with the other primates and with some fishes, reptiles, birds and insects, is essentially functional. It has evolved as a part of the visual system that goes beyond the basic capacity of most animals to detect contrast and movement to a level of much greater refinement and flexibility. This includes the ability not only to discriminate between different colours, but to respond to them as a means of conveying information, stimulating emotions and practising deception. These strategic functions and the colour sources that activate them are distinct from the incidental appearance of colour in the light of the sky, caused by the scattering of the short blue wavelengths of light.

Blue-green canophytes, primitive precursors of the algae that lived in the sea some three billion years ago, contained chlorophyll, which enabled them to use water in the photosynthetic process. Their ability to use energy from the sun to convert carbon dioxide and water into glucose and oxygen was a major advance in evolution, beginning the process of creating both the oxygen-rich atmosphere necessary for life and the ozone layer that protects us from ultraviolet radiation — the same rays that had produced energy to synthesise amino acids and sugars in the primordial oceans. Similar related species still exist. The floating blue-green *Trichodesium erythraeum* contains the pigment *phycorythrin,* which absorbs yellow, green, blue and violet light to produce the energy for the photochemical reactions that keep the plant alive. When it dies off it turns the sea water a reddish-brown colour; this is the origin of the name the Red Sea.

The reason for the greenness of plants is similar. Chlorophyll enables them to absorb the red, yellow, blue and violet wavelengths of light in sunlight, reflecting green as a part of the process of harnessing energy. In deciduous trees when the chlorophyll needed for photosynthesis breaks down in the autumn it allows red and yellow pigments based on

ABOVE: The exploitation of optical effects is derived originally from natural camouflage, such as the stripes of the zebra, which conceal it in the shimmering grasslands; BELOW: 'Dazzle-painting' was developed by the French navy during the First World War to give the impression that ships were sailing in different directions and was associated with the Vorticist Movement and Edward Wadsworth in England, and later produced echoes in Op Art and the work of Bridget Riley. Although the principle has been developed virtually everywhere for military purposes — most obviously in the irregular patterns of greens and browns applied to uniforms — the opportunities for application to buildings have generally been neglected (courtesy of Scottish Arts Council)

carotene and other substances to take over, changing the colours of the leaves before they fall. These colours are incidental by-products of the chemistry of life.

By contrast, both physically and visually, the evolution of flowers occurred like a gift to transform the face of the natural world. The major handicap of plants was that they were stationary. As flowers evolved some 150 million years ago plants were enabled to advertise their attractions to insects and birds, which would carry their fertilising pollen from one plant to another, sometimes over great distances. Correspondingly, colour vision developed in insects, which themselves evolved patterns and colours of extraordinary complexity to attract one another and to delude and repel their natural predators, the birds, reptiles and fish.

*Signal Functions of Colour in Nature*

Some signal functions — as for example the light signals emitted by glow-worms, fireflies and many species of fish — can be very direct. The message might be a simple one of attraction, as displayed in the yellow maw of a fledgling bird or the red spot on a gull's beak. As the colours of flowers attract pollinating insects seeking nectar, so those of fruits attract seed-eating birds. Warning messages are often more complicated, being conveyed by colour, pattern and frequently behaviour. Red and yellow are the most usual, appearing, for example, as the predominant colours of poisonous tree frogs and stinging insects. Red is also a prominent colour in the aggressive and courtship displays of many birds and animals, particularly apes. It also has a strong significance for man.

Concealment and mimicry are endemic to nature, and almost all creatures resort to some kind of deception to protect themselves. Of particular interest is the way in which some animals, birds and insects can blend with their backgrounds because of their pattern and colour. The stripes of a zebra, the spots of a leopard or the patterns of a giraffe might seem surprisingly regular, but they merge easily into the shimmering landscape of the savannah. Background colours also play an important part in the concealment of many reptiles, birds and insects. In these it is not uncommon to see a bold almost formal pattern detach itself visually (by virtue of being highly light-reflective) from a background of mottled browns and greys that blend perfectly into the vegetation. Such camouflage is the inspiration for some human disguises, for example, tribal masks in which geometric patterns are often used to distract from and so conceal the real form.

The principle of camouflage was developed during the First World War by a group of artists serving in a French battery at the end of 1914. Instead of consciously trying to mimic nature, they resorted to abstract painting. This led to the formation of a 'Section de Camouflage' in 1915, and two years later the technique was adopted by the British navy. 'Dazzle-painting', as it was called, used bold abstract stripes of black, white and blue paint to transform the great grey battleships, so that from quite a short distance it was impossible to tell in which direction they were steaming. The method, an off-shoot of Cubism that developed into Vorticism, interpreted reflections of sea and sky in ways that are highly relevant to our problems of manipulating the forms of buildings.[6]

*Colour Vision in Human Beings*
As hunters and food gatherers humans depended on their senses for survival in a potentially hostile environment. While the visual system generally played a dominant role in activity and the detection of movement, close colour vision was necessary for seeking out berries and other foodstuffs and examining them to ensure that they were edible and fresh. In spite of the diminution of these instinctive responses, humans still display a remarkable ability to discriminate by colour between the edible and the inedible, and to notice when a close associate appears healthy or 'off colour'.

The human eye, sometimes described as 'an outgrowth of the brain',[7] contains about 120 million rod-shaped cells that are sensitive only to light, and about 6 million cone-shaped cells that are responsive to colour; these are connected by the optic fibres to a series of nerve centres associated with the visual cortex in the brain. The rods are distributed generally over the surface of the retina, where the cones are rather sparse. The cones are concentrated towards the central area, particularly in the small centre (about 2 millimetres in diameter) called the fovea, where about 100,000 of them are so tightly packed that they look like rods.[8] The foveal region gives both the best detail and colour, although curiously it is less sensitive to low levels of light than the more primitive rod regions of the retina. Astronomers 'look off' the fovea when they wish to detect very faint stars, to allow light to fall on a region of the retina rich in sensitive rods. In this there is perhaps a hint of the evolution of human vision:

> . . . by moving from the centre of the human retina to its periphery we travel back in evolutionary time: from the most highly organised structure to a primitive eye, which does little more than detect move-

ments of shadows. The very edge of the human retina does not even give a sensation when stimulated by movement. It gives primitive unconscious vision; and directs the highly-developed foveal region to where it is likely to be needed for its high acuity.[9]

*Human Adaptations of Colour*

Given that there are such distinct physical as well as chromatic differences between colour or daylight ('photopic') vision and black-and-white or night-time ('scotopic') vision, and that we are able to switch from one to the other, it is interesting to have some insight into the loss of the former. This has been described by the neurologist Oliver Sacks in *The Case of the Colour-Blind Painter. An Anthropologist on Mars*.[10] His patient was a successful painter who at the age of sixty-five was involved in a motor accident in which he suffered an injury to his brain, resulting in the total loss of colour vision and the ability to visualise colour in memory and dreams. His first reaction was one of extreme horror. It was not just that colours were missing but that everything had 'a distasteful, dirty look: the whites glaring, yet discoloured and off-white; the blacks cavernous; everything wrong, unnatural, stained and impure'. Flesh was an abhorrent grey; 'flesh-coloured' had become 'rat-coloured'; and people appeared like 'animated grey statues'. The effect can perhaps be judged from that curious surreal painting by René Magritte, *Souvenir de Voyage III* (ADAGP, Paris),[11] in which he has portrayed a table with a tablecloth, a bowl of fruit and a bottle of wine, on a wooden floor by an open window, against the background of a rugged cliff. Everything is painted as if carved in one piece from the pitted grey rock of the cliff, united by the material but also by the deadly absence of colour.

Gradually the initial sense of helplessness began to leave Sacks' patient, giving way to a new sense of resolution: if he could not paint in colour he would paint in black and white. His resolution was strengthened by a singular experience that occurred about five weeks after the accident when he saw the sun rising over the highway. The blazing reds had all turned into black. 'The sun rose like a bomb, like some enormous nuclear explosion. Had anyone ever seen a sunrise in this way before?' After a year or more of experimentation he again became successful, and the change to painting in black and white was accepted as a natural phase of his artistic development.[12]

This painter's experience seems to have been curiously and perversely rewarding in enabling him to show the extraordinary human ability to accept misfortune and adapt to circumstances. It also emphasises the

*OPPOSITE L, FROM ABOVE: Winfrith Technology Centre, Dorset (colour design: Nicholas Pearson Associates)*
In the proposed rehabilitation of this 1950s nuclear research centre, located in a large area of Dorset heathland, two aims were identified: to integrate the buildings with the site when seen from a distance, and to improve their visual image at close quarters. A series of colour studies were made from different positions in the surrounding landscape, which included mixed farmland, broadleaf woodland, coniferous woodland, heathland and parkland. Colour boards were made and tested on site, allowing for seasonal changes. These provided the basis for a palette, from which a colour strategy was prepared, aimed specifically at reducing the effect of 'clutter' in the middle areas, and emphasising some of the smaller elements. Strong colours were suggested by the heath landscape, including the pinks and purples of heather, vivid yellow of gorse, and bracken changing from bright green to flame red — all seen against the duller browns and greens of the distant landscape. Applied to the Zebra building, the selected colours of dark red, orange-yellow and dark brown, highlighted with bright pinks appear fresh and lively in the near view; but in the middle and far distance, they blend very effectively with the landscape

*OPPOSITE R, ABOVE AND CENTRE: Fawley Power Station, Southampton Water (design: Farmer & Dark)*
Applications of colour derived from 'dazzle-painting' or camouflage techniques can be very effective in reducing the effect of bulk. In this example the almost achromatic greys, white and black, as well as the orange accent colour of the doors, were suggested by the colours of the shingle. It distracts from the 'clutter' of the surroundings and the colours relate well to the changing colours of sea and sky

*OPPOSITE R, BELOW: Partington Storage Tanks, Greater Manchester (design: Faulks, Perry, Culley & Rech)*
To reduce the effect of bulking and to add interest the tanks have been painted with graded vertical banding in red, purple, white and silver, relating differently to the three types of surrounding landscape character: rural, housing, and industry

interdependence of what tend to be thought of as two kinds of vision. This is reinforced by our object-centred learning. As infants we learn to recognise and handle shapes and forms as a means of exploring space. Although they reflect colour and this is appreciated by young children who have excellent discrimination, they 'are remarkably poor at talking about colour'.[13] The ability seems to depend upon objects with colour names, such as oranges, the metals gold and silver and paints. Coloured paints are viewed as distinct from the achromatic black and white — a distinction that continues with our experience of coloured and black-and-white drawings, photographs, films and television and the facility with which we can change from one mode to the other and back. The ability to move in and out of colour-vision mode is almost certainly adaptive, an aspect of our ability to adjust visually to the daily changing of the light. This enables us also to adapt to the extreme differences between a sunlit street and a dark room almost instantaneously — an adjustment in terms of light of about 100:1.[14] This ability, in common with other intuitions that we are inclined to regard as phobias, such as a fear of the dark, must have been important for survival in the past. Twilight is a dangerous time, when the light changes, predators emerge and fatigue is beginning to set in. It is also marked by a shift in colour perceptions, when red turns black and blues appear much stronger — known as the Purkinje Shift after the nineteenth-century Czech physiologist Jan Purkinje. This alteration in vision optimises reception from moonlight when light levels are too low to gain any advantage from colour.

In considering this form of adaptation and other factors (such as our predilection for certain colour words) in the light of certain conditions of evolution in the expanding universe, the cosmologist John D Barrow concludes:

> Atmospheric influences alone could thus have begun a sequence of adaptations because of the selective advantage conferred by genes that promote the development of neural processing for distinguishing simultaneously, and economically, the three colour variations.[15]

# FROM EVOLUTION TO REVOLUTION

The long and slow evolution of colour awareness and use can be judged from three sources: from its use in art and culture, from the much later development of language, and from anthropology, which forms a bridge between them. We tend to think of colour as a cultural factor, but the facts seem to suggest that it has evolved because it is important ecologically. The basic categories and values of colour are aspects of brain embryology and evolution, which could not have been learned. As infants we perceive certain universal truths that form the basis for communicating and using colour in different cultures.[16] The evolution of colour vision is dependent on the fact that the spectral composition of light in different environments has predictable values for human and animal life, one of which is the complementary composition of sunlight and shadows.[17] Goethe observed that under a yellow sun shadows appeared to be blue: 'In nature, reflections of the sky on the surface of water, or the shiny surfaces of leaves . . . are blue. Substance, particularly organic substance, is red, brown or yellowish . . . '[18] It seems likely that the ancient dichromatic visual system in the mid-brain enables us to appreciate the way blue space and reddish substance are distributed in the world before the more discriminating full-colour vision makes its contribution to perception of detail.

> Every fruit-eating bird or monkey knows how to tell ripe, sugar-laden berries by their colour. Bright reds and yellows signal sweetness to birds and mammals. The same colours are effective socially in courtship and threat — they, with bold stripes and spots, may also be markers of organic poisons.[19]

The idea seems to gain support from the study of colour words in ninety-eight different languages undertaken by two American anthropologists, Brent Berlin and Paul Kay. From the total of eleven common colour words only two are found in all the languages. No language has only one colour word; there are always two or more, and the two are always black and white. If there are three, the third is always red. When there are four, green or yellow is added, and both are included when there are five. If there are six, blue is one of them, and if seven, brown.

Eight or more include purple, pink, orange and grey, but not necessarily in that order. So strict are the limitations that out of 2048 possible combinations of the 11 colour words only 22 are found.[20]

The last group of colours, purple, pink, orange and grey, are among those most associated with the more advanced societies, which use the largest numbers of colour words. It is significant also that these (apart from grey) are the more exotic colours, found naturally in the deep sea and now often used to create dramatic effects that may appear intrusive (see Colour Strategies). Unexpected, unnatural or negative ways of using colour, for example when an orange is depicted as blue or a rose as green, cause a curious sense of revulsion, but it is often precisely this artificiality that is exploited by artists and designers wishing to capture attention.[21]

The Kikuyu language of Kenya includes colour words only for black, white and red, associated locally with references to soot, teeth and blood, and more universally with darkness and light and the fundamental experiences of living. White and black are also commonly representative of good and evil, innocence and guilt, life and death, and redness represents blood, the body, birth, love, and conflict. It is also, with the associated yellows and browns, the colour of earth, rocks and building materials.

If we think of the world in terms of zones of colour — the blue of the sky and its reflection from water, the greens of vegetation and the warm reddish colours of the earth — it is for the latter that we seem to have a predisposition. Availability must play a part in this; blue and green minerals are rare in nature, while red and yellow ochres are ubiquitous. It is no coincidence that the latter feature most frequently in the arts and crafts of traditional societies; they are also the colours of ice-age paintings.

Painting that we can recognise as art for its extraordinarily vital images of mammoth, deer, wild cattle, horses and bison, has been found in caves scattered along the edge of the European ice sheet, currently dated between c 34000BC and c 15000BC. The colours used were red, yellow-orange and brown ochres from the earth, and brown and black from carbon and manganese (which turns bluish). The paintings are superimposed, many of them placed awkwardly in caves that could only have been reached by hours of crawling. They were painted by the light of flickering stone lamps filled with animal fat, with brushes made from burred sticks or with the fingers — and occasionally by blowing paint directly on to the rock. The most plausible explanation for their presence is that of sympathetic magic, to ensure success in the hunt, but this is partially discounted by the fact that the bones found in the caves were of different species of animals from those portrayed.[22] Whatever the reason, they are a clear and astonishing record of human achievement — of the ability to visualise experience and pass it on to future generations, thus linking past, present and future. This is a uniquely human talent, expressed through both the arts and the sciences, from simple tools to elaborate machines and from 'primitive' paintings to television.[23]

*Colour Symbolism*

Colour symbolism permeates our lives in a variety of ways. The rituals of birth, coming of age, marriage and death are celebrated by the use of symbolic colours, which vary from one society to another. The practice of personal adornment continues in both 'pre-industrial' and developed societies, along with the decoration of possessions, houses and sur-roundings. Significantly there is also still a predominance of the three basic colours (white, black and red) that have been in use since before the ice ages. White and black still symbolise life and death, although in India and the East white rather than black is the symbol of mourning. Red commonly represents love, passion, blood, heat, war, fire and dan-ger. In China it is the symbol of good fortune. In writing about revolu-tionary China, Yung Chang relates how a group of over-enthusiastic Red Guards reasoned that the colour red should be associated with activity. Accordingly, they changed the order of the traffic lights so that red signified 'go'. Unfortunately, they did not change them all. A more sinister act was the blackening of professors' faces to symbolise evil.[25]

These examples illustrate the common confusion or conflict between colour symbolism and the uses of colour that are clearly — even liter-ally in the first case — signal functions, and symbolism. All are mean-ingful, but only in relation to context and the viewer's perceptual priori-ties at the time. The confusion indicates both how far we have moved from our biological and social roots and how necessary it is to take a new look and establish a balanced view in response to the needs and pressures of the present.

*Colour and Industry*

The modern colour revolution has its origins in the division of light into the spectral colours by Isaac Newton in 1669. Speculation about the precise nature of light energy and the essential differences between wavelengths continued for three hundred years afterwards,[26] and the confusion between light and pigment colours was still hampering research during the first half of the nineteenth century.[27] As far as the general understanding of colour is concerned, the confusion remains (see next chapter).

The nineteenth century was distinguished by major advances in science and industry in England, Germany and France in particular, including the development in France, from the end of the eighteenth century onwards, of a new systematic form of chemistry. Chemical research produced a large number of new pigments based on metals (chromium, cadmium, cobalt, zinc, copper and arsenic), resulting in new bright colours that were later to form the basis of the Impressionist palette.[28] With mechanisation and the much wider uses of colour and paint came the need for measurement. This was undertaken by, among others, Michel Eugène Chevreul on his appointment in 1824 as Director of Dyeing of the Gobelins tapestry factory in Paris. One of his first tasks was to rationalise the many thousands of dyes then in use into an organised system of 1,500, derived from twelve principal colours.[29] From this experience he went on to develop principles of colour harmony, which he applied to the uses of colour in a range of different fields from painting and textiles to architecture and horticulture. Moreover, he provided explanations for such peculiarities as optical mixing and simultaneous contrast (see Glossary). In pointing out that orange sunlight induced violet shadows, Chevreul offered invaluable guidance to the Impressionist painters, providing an argument against those who were suspicious of the sensory approach to colour.

Colour printing had made it possible to publish lithographic reproductions in colour. Reproductions by Hitorff, based upon archaeological evidence, enabled people to see for the first time how the temples of classical Greece had looked when they were painted. In 1856 the architect Owen Jones published *The Grammar of Ornament*, demonstrating the vital role that colour had played in the cultures of different parts of the world and including 'the ornament of savage tribes'.[30] Although his ideas were somewhat confused by his belief that the use of primary colours characterised high points in civilisations (with the mediocre and low points being marked by secondary and tertiary colours; see Glossary), he was wise enough to advocate art education for all: artists, manufacturers and the public. In his major colour project, as superintendent of works for the Great Exhibition (1851) at the Crystal Palace, he specified blue and white for the exterior framework or struc-

*OPPOSITE: The Forth Railway Bridge, Scotland. Protection was the first criterion when iron and steel began to be used for bridges in the eighteenth century, and plans to paint the Golden Gate Bridge in San Francisco gold to commemorate the Gold Rush (1849) were abandoned in favour of red lead oxide. This was also used for the Forth Bridge. The red is a good landscape colour, which works well with rocks, earth and green fields, as well as buildings. Modern bridges are generally protected with a labour-saving metallic coating to avoid the need for painting, but the principle of allowing the iron to rust naturally as both a protective and a decorative coating has been applied to a number of buildings*

ture and red, yellow and blue with white for the interior; the latter group combined in a subtle form of optical mixing. On engineering structures, which were not regarded as architecture, such profligate use of colour was occasionally allowed. Architecture was considered to include the frontages but not the sooty trainsheds of railway stations and was still under the spell of Ruskin's dictum requiring the use of self-coloured materials. This was derived from the Gothic but reinforced by neoclassicism, as it was to be again reinforced by the doctrines of the modern movements. Yet cast iron and steel needed paint for protection, and the increasing number of bridges and other edifices were providing opportunities for creative or at least strategic uses of colour. In fact, only in the postwar years of the twentieth century have these opportunities been exploited to any considerable degree. The reds used on the Forth Railway Bridge and on the Golden Gate Bridge, San Francisco, might be described as good landscape colours, particularly suitable in contrast to the greens of vegetation; they were originally made with lead oxide, chosen for its preservative qualities rather than the colour. Perhaps there is a deeper logic here — a rationalism that derives from nature.

Of all the revolutionary developments the most significant was that of synthesis, the creation of colours by chemical means. This had been achieved at various times, for example, in the creation in Berlin (1704) of Prussian blue, a valuable complement to the rare ultramarine, but the process began seriously in the 1860s. At that time there were only a few hundred colours of vegetable, animal and mineral origin in common use. In 1856 a pupil of the German chemist Hofmann, experimenting with quinine, had produced a black sludge, which he discovered on examination to be a beautiful dye that was resistant to both water and light. The French called it 'mauve' after the mallow plant, and the colour was fashionable for a decade (Queen Victoria wore a mauve dress in 1862). It was the first of thousands of dyes synthesised from petroleum and other chemical compounds. By 1980 the number had reached three million, of which some nine thousand had appeared on the market. Considering this situation and noting the large ranges of paint colours that have now become available (not to mention colours in plastics and other materials), it may seem surprising that the 'colour revolution' has been so slow in its effect.[31]

# THE NATURE OF COLOUR

Colour appearance in the environment depends on three variables: light, surface and distance, each of which is to some extent within our control. We can control the light by means of orientation and alignment, and we can use artificial sources; we can control the surface in terms of size, shape, texture and pigmentation; and we can manipulate the views according to the distances from which they are seen.

## Colour and Light

Colour is light made visible through interaction with surfaces of all kinds. It is the surfaces — whether they are opaque or translucent — that make colour visible. Their pigmentation determines which colours are absorbed, which transmitted or refracted and which reflected. It is assumed that people with normal vision see more or less the same colours, with slight variations. The light may be natural in the form of sunlight, moonlight or starlight or artificial in the form of incandescent filament or fluorescent light; each has its own characteristics. Natural daylight comprises both direct sunlight and the reflected light of the sky. Sunlight shares characteristics with filament and other fixed-point light sources in highlighting surfaces and casting deep shadows, which accentuate form and texture. The light of the sky is diffused, resembling the light from fluorescent lamps and producing only weak shadows. The proportion of sunlight to reflected sky light varies according to the location, the time of day, and the atmospheric conditions. Mist and cloud, dust and atmospheric pollution cause the light to be diffused. The apparent blueness of the sky is produced by atmospheric particles, which scatter the sunlight. This affects mostly the shorter wavelengths, making the sky appear as a mixture of violet (to which our eyes are not very sensitive), blue, a little green and very small quantities of yellow and red. A similar effect of blueness occurs in the view of distant mountains and in the smoke of a bonfire seen against a dark background (against a light background it looks yellowish). The presence of atmospheric dust dilutes the blue of the sky, giving it the whitish appearance typical of large cities.

The variable coloured light of the rainbow, which is the source of our theories of colour, is caused by low sunlight penetrating drops of water. The light rays are split by refraction and then reflected back to the observer at the rainbow angle of 41-42 degrees. When the raindrops are large enough to reflect the light rays twice before they emerge a secondary bow is seen at an angle of 52-54 degrees. It is always fainter than the primary rainbow because some of the light escapes.[31] Artificial rainbows can be created in the laboratory, and various attempts have been made to create them out of doors.

## Colour and Surface

Textured surfaces reflect diffusely; smooth surfaces reflect directly — always subject to the relative angles of the light source and the observer. Textures vary with scale and distance: for example, the texture of a rough surface at close quarters may have an effect equivalent to that of a ribbed material further away or even a row of bay windows in the distance. Their colour would vary both according to the atmospheric effect of the distance and the mixture of colours visible, including shadows, through the process of colour assimilation or optical mixing. Wet surfaces and smooth materials reflect more intensely than dry or rough ones; for example, gloss paint reflects colour more intensely than matt. This is the reason why glazed ceramic tiles make a much stronger visual impact than unglazed tiles or concrete and why glazed and varnished pictures are so difficult to hang. Differences in texture can be fundamental in the distinction between the old and the new or between the natural and the manufactured — for it is perhaps texture above all that distinguishes nature.

The pigmentation contained within any material — whether it be natural or artificial — determines the colour by its capacity to absorb a proportion of the constituent colours of natural light (the additive primary colours: orange-red, green and blue-violet;[32] see Glossary). A flower appears yellow in daylight because it absorbs the blue-violet content of white light, reflecting a mixture of orange-red and green, which makes yellow. A leaf that looks green is absorbing the orange-red and blue-violet wavelengths. A surface that reflects all three wavelengths will appear white, and one that absorbs them all will appear black.[33] In practice, such purity scarcely exists — as we can judge from walking through 'white' towns and villages (see Colour and Place) — and the polarities of pure black and pure white are generally excluded from paint colour systems. (It is, however, possible to achieve about 98%

OPPOSITE AND ABOVE: Venice.
*'The coloured phantoms of the buildings of Venice, floating on a watery surface, seem to be lighter than all other houses one has ever seen . . . These light palaces are not, like other buildings, characterised by certain architectural elements that are supporting and others that are supported. They are simply divided by narrow mouldings, twisted like cords or decorated like borders, and between the mouldings are stretched the colour planes of the facades . . . ' (SE Rasmussen)*

COLOURSCAPE

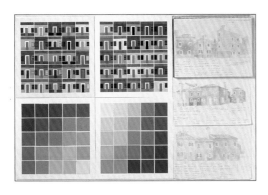

*ABOVE: Colour analysis of Burano, Italy, by J-P Lenclos*

*OPPOSITE: Burano, Italy.*
*The island of Burano across the lagoon must be one of the most frequently illustrated examples of 'indigenous' or vernacular colour. It is quite different from Venice, lacking the sense of the passage of time in the fading earth pigments of the mother city. The Buranelli people are also reputedly different, descended according to tradition either from a tribe of people who originated in Asia Minor or, more likely, from the galley slaves who were quartered in Burano during the Venetian wars. Their sense of independence extends to the painting of their houses. According to Shirley Guiton, offers of free paint by the Soprintendenza di Monumenti and advice on 'a harmonious colour scheme' were ignored; the owners 'paint their houses early in the morning before the authorities come round on their visits'. The surprising fact is that they manage successfully to achieve a harmonious impression using so many strong colours, unified only by the consistent use of white for door and window surrounds and green for the shutters*

reflection from a coating of magnesium oxide on cold metal and a 97% absorption with carbon black.)[34] In the 1990s the fashion for 'brilliant' white (which will reflect about 90% of the light) and other luminescent colours excluded from paint colour swatches does not prevent the development and use of newer brighter colours or of metallic surfaces.

Natural materials, like nature itself, tend to be richly textured and subtly coloured. If such variations do not occur in the material itself — and many types of stone are very plain — the deficiency has often been made up in the detail of traditional building. Similar principles apply to small-unit manufactured materials, such as bricks. However, the historian Alec Clifton-Taylor gave a word of warning about the bricks made with the clay from a certain deep seam revealed in drilling for coal, which are called 'Accrington bloods' in allusion to their smooth bright pink complexion.[35] Whether or not there is an unseen relationship between site and materials — a kind of natural integrity as some believe — there are undoubtedly good reasons for avoiding some materials. Victor Pasmore deliberately rejected the local traditional brick for his housing in Peterlee new town because he believed it to be too strong a colour for large-scale use. His choice of a dark brown brick used in an uncompromisingly modern way appropriately bridged the gap between old and new, and he was realistic, if gloomy, about the decline of the vernacular tradition, predicting that:

> . . . architecture will finally lose all its basic natural connections except in marginal form. Out altogether . . . will go the country town clinging to the hillside or nestling in a valley with its walls built of the natural stone on which it stands and the timber by which it is surrounded. Prefabrication and synthetic material make such an intimate relationship out of the question. It is this increasing erosion of naturalism in building construction which leaves the door open for a colour revolution in architecture.[36]

The development of new materials, including paints, can be seen in terms of the pursuit of precision, which in the machine age can be read as perfection. Modern materials tend to be sleek, smooth, functional and easily reproducible; paints are required to be weatherproof, colourfast and durable. These conditions are far removed from the traditions in which all aspects of an environment, both natural and human, incorporated irregularities. Those influencing 'market forces' have not been unaware of this problem, but the solution has been perceived much more in terms of attempts to manufacture and reproduce the artefacts of the past — in architectural pastiche — than to capture their

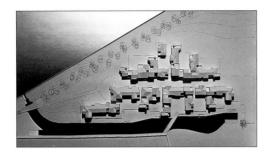

*ABOVE AND OPPOSITE: Mazzorbo, Italy. Giancarlo de Carlo, the architect of the new houses in Mazzorbo, wisely avoided the temptation to imitate either the ancient tradition of earth colours that distinguishes Venice or the dramatic colour of the adjoining island of Burano. Instead he chose a cooler, lighter range of blues, greens and yellow ochre, varying their intensities to give an impression of unity and contrast without going so far as to articulate each house. The initial idea of leaving the inhabitants free to colour their own houses was discounted because the process of development for the new houses was completely different from the traditional one and it was considered more appropriate to follow the same process through consistently. An analysis was done on the 'chromatic structures' existing in Burano and Mazzorbo; then, through many tests, drawings and samples and accurate observations (at different hours of the day, with bright and cloudy sky, in sun and rain), it was decided to use three different tonalities of three different colours: green, yellow and purple. Instead of differentiating the units, the different tonalities of the same colour mark the various planes composing the facade of each house. 'It might be that in the future the inhabitants will repaint the buildings differently and will thus distinguish their own house from the others, but by then they will have developed a sense of identity with their houses that cannot yet exist' (Giancarlo de Carlo)*

essence. There are, however, some encouraging signs, particularly in the field of colour.

The term modern materials refers to self-coloured materials, such as metal and glass, plastics and paint used in the new structures that are associated most readily with Modernism and Postmodernism. These include towers and high-rise slab-blocks, industrial sheds and other less collectively identifiable building types. Common features include a high degree of reflective material in the form of mirror-glass, glass and metals, combined with highly reflective saturated and luminous colours. Among the many advantages of such high-tech structures is their immaculate appearance, but they tend to preclude competition. In the cities they are often at odds with the older urban fabric; on the urban fringe they jockey for commercial advantage; and in the country they exhibit the same disadvantages that used to be attributed to asbestos-cement roofs in Britain — they do not appear to belong. In some cases the problem has been solved by uniform industrial estates and 'science parks'. In the new city of Milton Keynes, large numbers of 'units of accommodation' were fitted into a series of giant metal sheds, all similarly coloured a strong eye-catching but unifying yellow.

Paradoxically, it is white, which we do not think of as a colour, that is the most intrusive colour in our surroundings. This is because of its eye-catching quality owing to a high degree of light reflection — a quality shared by the many thousands of light and 'pastel' colours — and to its ubiquity. A single white farmhouse on a mountainside is a symbol of isolated security — a haven — but rows of white suburban houses disrupt the compact image of the village. White litter of papers, plastics, notices, caravans, bungalows and houses produces a picture of visual chaos. But the achromatic white is also the colour of order when we consider the white villages of the Mediterranean, the white terraces of Bayswater and the way that the colour reinforces the fronts of river and seaside towns in Britain.

### Colour and Distance

White remains visible for long distances — an advantage both in the use of camouflage techniques on buildings and for reducing the effect of towers seen against the whitish skies that are prevalent in many countries. The 'advancing' characteristics of bright reflective yellow and orange used for sea rescue services are also visible at a distance, but other colours, such as red, quickly darken. Colours begin to merge with one another and the colour distinction between painted surfaces and

natural materials disappears at a relatively short distance when textures are no longer discernible. Even the distinctive colours and textures of bricks and their mortar mix optically when viewed from the middle distance, coalescing into a uniform colour. This process of colour assimilation continues as the distance increases, the colours of objects becoming more assimilated and more closely related to each other until they merge into the bluish grey of the distance.

In a particular measured experiment in Sweden, Anders Hard observed that leaves which at close quarters appeared yellowish green looked blackish green from further away and then bluish green, but with decreasing intensity. At a distance of about 1.6 kilometres (1 mile), the colour had become a whitish grey, grading away to a reddish blue at some 16 kilometres (10 miles) distance. The effect, which is variable according to the weather and light conditions, is attributed generally to the scattering of blue light, known to painters as aerial perspective and expressed in such names as the Blue Ridge Mountains.

The architect and writer Steen Eiler Rasmussen compares the view of Manhattan from the deck of a ship over thirteen miles of water — 'like the painted back-drop of a theatre', with outlines but no impression of depth — with that of Venice:

> Coming from the Adriatic, which forms a dramatic seascape of wave crests with shadows of an amazingly intense ultramarine, to the flat waters of the lagoons behind the string of islands, you feel that you have been transported to an unreal world where the usual concepts of shape and form have lost their meaning. Sky and water merge into a brilliant blue sphere in the middle of which dark fishing boats glide and the low islands appear simply as floating horizontal stripes . . . [37]

# COLOUR PERCEPTION

*Ways of Seeing*

We perceive colour principally in two different ways: as an attribute of objects and as a separate sensory phenomenon. The surprising fact is that the first, regarded as natural and normal, is based not upon the true appearance of the colours but upon our experience and visual memory — what we have learnt rather than what we actually see. We know that the sky is blue, that the grass is green and that the earth is brown. The true or sensory view of colours is generally regarded as the prerogative of painters and others who work with colour. For most of us, most of the time, it is the 'object view' that prevails.

In order to negotiate objects and find our way in the world, we need to be able to identify things (and people) under a variety of different circumstances and in different light conditions. In parallel with constancies of size, shape, texture and brightness, colour constancy (see Glossary) enables us to recognise objects and situations that experience has taught us to identify, thus freeing our perceptual faculties for the detection of the new and the less familiar. In this there is a direct similarity between the brain and the information processing mechanism of a computer, although the former is infinitely more sophisticated. The visual system is adapted to obtaining a maximum of information with a minimum of effort; that which is not immediately required or can be taken for granted, can be considered redundant: 'the eye has evolved to see the world in unchanging colour, regardless of always unpredictable, shifting and uneven illumination.'[38]

Colour for Newton and the classical theorists, was something local and absolute, given by the wavelength of light reflected from each point. Edwin Land, however, has demonstrated that colour perception is neither local nor absolute but determined by comparisons of the wavelength composition of light reflected from each point with that of its surround, on the basis of surveying the whole scene.[39] It depends upon a continuous process of relating and comparing. Whereas previous models for colour classification (see In Search of Harmony) had been based on the concept of colour addition, expressed as triangles, spheres and

ABOVE: Most people see only six distinct colours in the rainbow. Newton, relying on the eyes of an assistant, gave it seven, thus relating it to the seven known planets and the seven notes of the diatonic scale. It is caused by low sunlight penetrating drops of water. A secondary bow is seen when the raindrops are large enough to reflect the light rays twice

circular solids, Land's model was one of comparison, expressed in the form of a colour cube. He proposed two sets of comparisons: first, of the reflectance of all surfaces in a scene within a certain waveband (group of wavelengths), which he described as a 'lightness record'; second, a comparison of the three separate lightness records for the wavebands corresponding roughly to the red, green and blue wavelengths. These two sets of values determined the colours perceived. Land was careful to avoid locating any particular brain site for the process, using the name 'Retinex' to infer a range of sites between the retina and the visual cortex.[40]

The apparent dichotomy of colour vision, which may be owing to evaluation mechanisms operating at different sites within the visual system, may give answers to a number of questions that arise in attempting to analyse visual perception. First it must surely account for the fact that so many people seem genuinely unresponsive to colour, compared with those whom we credit with aptitude, intuition or flair. It might well account for the common tendency to look at paintings in art galleries without registering their colours and explain why painters can be divided between those whom we regard as 'good colourists' and those for whom the subject and the academic process is more important. There is, for example, a long-standing distinction between those schools of painting based upon drawing, such as the Florentine, and those for which colour was predominant, such as the Venetian. This situation still persists today in the division between the objective and the sensory ways of viewing. The painter Patrick Heron summarises neatly with his comment, 'the realities of the senses are no longer self-evident (strange as it may seem) to the majority . . . '[41]

The official academic viewpoint was that painting had to portray something in particular. The painter Jean Auguste Dominique Ingres wrote, ' . . . drawing is everything, the whole of art lies there. The material processes of painting are very easy and can be learnt in a week or so.'[42] Such relegation of the subject to the level of a child's colouring book is not untypical and could well be applied to the study of colour in architecture today. There are probably three reasons for this, firstly the emphasis placed by the neoclassical tradition on the natural colours of materials; secondly the belief held by members of the modern movements that colour distorts form; and thirdly our objective habits of seeing.

Although we are only beginning to understand the mechanisms of the different types of perception, it seems clear that they are not mutually exclusive and it is likely that many intermediate stages exist. JJ Gibson distinguishes them by location: 'filmy disembodied colours floating in a *visual field*', compared with 'the colours of objective surfaces in a *visual world*.' The former look 'filmy and insubstantial and appear at an indefinite distance, in contrast with the colours of objects in daylight illumination which appear to be localised on and be part of the surface of the object in question.'[43]

Given that perception is a very selective activity concerned with much more than just appearances, it is necessary to consider how our concept of the visual world is formed. While it is clear that we can only survive in a functional environment, there is much disagreement on how these functions are expressed. Buildings, for example, are expected to be much more than forms following function. They are symbols, comforting or otherwise, of the places we live in. This raises the question of how a particular environment is perceived and, more specifically, how it contributes to our overall image of the world. The visual process is one of scanning. The eyes move, and so do the head, neck and body, gathering images like the frames of a moving film. From these images and other sensory impressions gathered simultaneously the scene is constructed in the light of information already stored in our visual memories, redundant or unnecessary information being filtered out.

To what extent cultural and social factors influence this 'editing' process it is impossible to assess. In view of the ways in which we exercise taste and discrimination in describing our surroundings, it would appear that the picture of the world on which these judgements are based is in many ways a product of our own imagination.

*Learning to See Colour*

Although the precise optical and neurological processes involved in seeing and perception are still under investigation, it is known that visual awareness can be developed. Learning to 'see' is a fundamental aspect of all courses in art and design, and it is a common complaint among practitioners that such education is not general. Even among specialists there are different priorities and interpretations relating to aspects of the visual world, of which colour is one of the most problematical.

The essential connection between colour and objects begins in infancy. As babies we are attracted by the lightness and brightness of things, but it is only later, probably with the beginning of the development of abstract concepts (facilitated by language), that we learn to

*ABOVE AND BELOW: The River Thames at Barnes (c1982). The everyday appearance of a landscape accustoms us to the local colours of scenes and objects, but these can change dramatically with the light*

perceive colour as a separate sensation. Observations of a group of children revealed those up to the age of two or two-and-a-half tended to match objects by shape rather than colour. The numbers who matched according to colour increased steadily up to about the age of four-and-a-half and then began to decrease.[44] After that age, as our culture increasingly demands training in practical skills that rely more heavily on shape than colour,[45] the priority given to colours normally decreases continuously into adulthood.[46] Considering that young children in the age group mentioned exhibit a strong sense of colour perception in their activities, which they have some difficulty in describing, we may wonder at their ability to come to terms with the colour confusion that surrounds the average child today.

Almost all of us have some capacity to see colour in a detached way. The blue of the sky, for example, is essentially filmy and insubstantial, like that of the layers of blue haze covering distant mountains. The colours of the rainbow, although produced by different means, have a similar quality. Most people are aware of the shimmering mirage-like appearance of objects and buildings seen at a distance. Rasmussen's comparison of Manhattan and Venice also exemplifies this detached way of seeing colour.[47] Such effects are typically expressed by the indistinct patches of colour in the paintings by Nicholas de Stael. There are close parallels also in 'dazzle-painting' (see The Purpose of Colour).

An impressive effect, in which natural light transforms the visual world from its ordinary appearance to one of glowing light and colour, occurs when the sun is low and the sky is dark with storm clouds. As the sun moves towards the horizon, the blue light, which is refracted at the sharpest angle, ceases to be visible, the only colours reaching the eye being those with the longer wavelengths — yellow and red. This intense red and yellow light turns everything to gold, transforming all objects. All colours are united in the harmony of a single dominant hue, contrasted with the dark blue-grey of the sky.[48]

# IN SEARCH OF HARMONY

Aristotle thought that rays of coloured light travelled through the air to the eye and into the body, 'where the intellect has intercourse with the soul'. The theories of the Greek philosophers and those of the medieval writers Robert Grosseteste, Leon Battista Alberti and Leonardo da Vinci together provided a basis for the large number of colour systems that began to develop in the seventeenth century. They were concerned in different ways, with different emphases, about the sources of colour, the way it was transmitted, the way it was received by the eyes and the ways in which it was interpreted by the brain. When Isaac Newton demonstrated in 1669-71 that white light could be split into the spectrum of colours he solved one problem,[49] but others remained: for instance, the question of how light was transmitted. Christian Huygens had pioneered the pulse theory of 'waves travelling through an aether', in opposition to the particle theory espoused by Newton. The matter was not settled until 1873, when the Scottish physicist James Clerk Maxwell discovered that light (and colour) constituted part of the electromagnetic system comprising gamma rays, X-rays, ultraviolet and infrared rays, microwaves, radar, radio and television waves.[50] Some radio waves are several hundred metres long, but the wavelengths of light are minute — so short that they can be measured only in nanometres (nm; 1 nanometre = $10^{-9}$ or 0.000000001 metre). Electromagnetic waves have four defining characteristics: velocity, frequency, amplitude and wavelength. This immediately places the subject beyond general comprehension — but not so its effects, in relation to which Aristotle's definition has a curiously prophetic ring.

*Colour Classification Systems*

An analysis of colour classification in *Idée Farbe* (1994) lists some sixty systems, starting with those of the Greek philosophers and the early Italian Renaissance and continuing with five each in the seventeenth and eighteenth centuries (the latter beginning with that of Isaac Newton's *Optics*, 1704), thirteen in the nineteenth century and the remainder in the twentieth. In addition there are twelve systems relating to

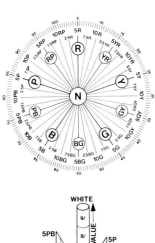

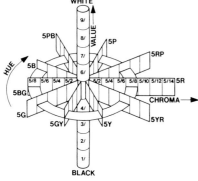

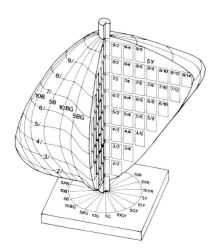

*FROM ABOVE: The Munsell system of colour notation: Related hue symbols arranged on a 100-hue circle; Hue, value and chroma scales arranged in colour space on a colour 'tree'; Munsell colour solid with one quarter removed to show constant hue 5Y (courtesy of DG Colour Ltd, Salisbury)*

religious, national and other traditions, including the Chinese, Indian, Hebrew and Islamic systems, and those based on symbolism, heraldry, anthroposophy and astrology.[51] This gives some idea of the volume of material that has served over the centuries both to clarify and explain the subject on the one hand and to cloud and confuse it with cultural and esoteric notions on the other. But it is well to remember that nature, science and alchemy had common roots. Newton did not see seven colours in the rainbow. Apparently, he saw only five in 1669, but relying upon a young assistant 'whose eyes for distinguishing colours were more critical than mine'[52] he raised the figure to seven in 1671, adding orange and indigo, the latter named after a colour from India that had become fashionable ('indigo' means Indian dye), to relate the spectrum to the seven notes of the diatonic scale and the seven known planets.

Classification systems began with simple geometric figures (squares, circles and triangles), showing the different hues in spectral sequence. In those based on the needs of painting, the pigment primary colours — red, yellow and blue[53] — were arranged with their secondaries — orange, green and purple — in between, and likewise with the tertiaries. The circular form achieved by joining the spectral edges of the rainbow, with purple between red and blue, lent itself to expansion from a basic six steps or divisions to accommodate over a hundred graduations of intensity of the different hues merging into one another.

Theorists began to identify three 'dimensions' of colour. 'Hue' is the generally accepted term for the colours resulting from the different wavelengths, although the word 'colour' is invariably used colloquially in this context, as it has been for convenience throughout this book. Every hue has its own saturation or intensity, ranging from the purest, most concentrated or 'saturated' to the most dilute; this is referred to as 'chroma' in the forty-step colour classification system devised by Munsell. Each colour also has its own degree of lightness, referred to as 'value' in the Munsell system (see Colour Effects). Three-dimensional models were required if, in addition to hue, colour classification systems were to represent both saturation and lightness. In general these models provided for lightness to be expressed on a scale running from top to bottom, for the hues to be arranged around the perimeter and for the degree of saturation to be expressed according to the distance from the axis at any level between white at the top and black at the bottom. In the Munsell system this arrangement is expressed by the figure of a tree with unequal branches; in the Natural Colour System (see below) it is expressed by a double cone.

A simple illustration of the measurement of coloured light is provided by the system of optical matching devised in 1880 by Joseph Lovibond, a Salisbury brewer, in response to complaints about the strength of his beer. Supposedly inspired by the stained glass in the cathedral, Lovibond had the idea of colour-testing the beer against a series of brown glass filters. The invention was so successful that he developed it into the Lovibond Tintometer, which until the late twentieth century was in use for distinguishing between nine million variations by means of different combinations of glass filters in magenta, yellow and cyan — the three subtractive primary colours for pigments and additive secondary colours for light (see Glossary).[54]

For environmental purposes the inevitable confusion between colours and the descriptions, terminology and systems applied to them in different contexts has to some extent been resolved by the Natural Colour System (NCS) of Sweden,[55] which depends particularly on the fundamental ways of perceiving and of using colour in the environment. This recognises the importance of the achromatic 'colours' black and white, together with yellow, red, blue and green as 'elementary' colours. Black, white and green are included because the system is based not on how colours are mixed, but on how they are perceived. The colour solid adopted for this system is a double cone with the polar axis extending from white to black, crossed in the middle by blue–yellow and red–green axes. An adaptation of Newton's colour sphere, it is a direct reflection of JD Barrow's views of the evolutionary basis of human colour perception (see The Purpose of Colour).[56]

There are differences not only among scientists in their attitudes to colour classification but also among psychologists with regard to colour perception. Johann Wolfgang von Goethe was one of the first to include subjective reactions in his colour theory. ME Chevreul demonstrated the universality of colour at about the same time (1839) by showing how the principles applied equally to everything from dyeing textiles, painting and stained glass to interior design, architecture and horticulture. In *De la Loi du Contraste Simultane des Couleurs* he identified six kinds of colour harmony: three of analogy and three of contrast.[57] These can be summarised as harmonies of adjacent, opposite, split-complementary and triadic colours, harmony of identity and that of a dominant hue. Most theorists agree with Chevreul's general observation that colours look best together either when they are closely related (analogous), or opposite (complementary), and this has been confirmed by a number of studies in psychology.

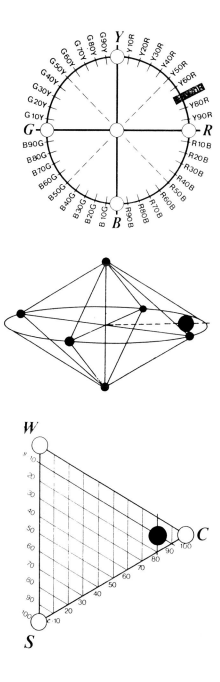

*FROM ABOVE: The Natural Colour System (NCS) as adopted by ICI: Colour circle; Colour figure; Colour triangle (courtesy of ICI)*

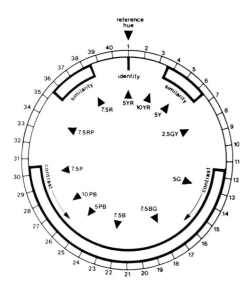

ABOVE: The hue-harmony selector.
The harmonies of identity, similarity and contrast,
separated by zones of ambiguity on a forty-step Munsell
hue scale. This diagram (based on Moon and Spencer,
1944) was developed by HL Gloag after detailed
investigations of five leading theorists on the subject of
harmony. The arrows show the relationship between one
of the main framework hues and the other eleven in the
BS 5252 Colour Co-ordination Framework (HMSO)

In a study of the work of five different theorists, which was published as *The Colour Co-ordination Handbook*,[58] HL Gloag and M Gold concluded that harmony was primarily associated with hue, in terms of 'a clear-cut unambiguous relationship', rather than with the lightness or saturation of colours. They constructed a 'hue-harmony selector' with a series of revolving discs indicating three types of harmony: of identity, of similarity and of contrast, each separated by zones of ambiguity on a forty-step Munsell hue scale. The selector was intended not as an arbiter but as a guide in the selection and coordination of hues; its readings have been found to coincide well with the judgements of designers. While much has been written about the principles of harmony relating to the three 'dimensions' of colour, the question of ambiguity has been neglected. It is this quality, this lack of resolution (perhaps in any field of design), that is disturbing. In colour it occurs frequently because of the complexities of accurate colour description. A common example is the use of green in the landscape. Green paint, because it is green, is commonly assumed to be suitable for buildings seen against a green background, for example, barns. To avoid ambiguity it is necessary to use a green that contrasts with the mixed greens of nature — for example a yellow-green or one that is very dark, or better still to follow traditional precedents and use colours that are more in contrast.

Fashion and usage undoubtedly play an important part in colour selection, and we may reflect on the stages of 'the colour revolution' that has occurred in the Western world during the nineteenth and twentieth centuries, dramatically increasing the range of colours available and inducing us to use the colour palettes of different cultures. The chemist Wilhelm Ostwald, who devised a colour system in 1916-17, perhaps fell into a similar trap to Owen Jones (see From Evolution to Revolution) when he condemned the large surfaces of pure vermilion found in Pompeii as crude and a discredit to the idea of the artistic superiority of the ancients.[59] Painters, with few exceptions, work from intuition: the physiologist and theorist Ewald Hering noted that many paintings contain inharmonious combinations, and Rudolf Arnheim cautiously suggested that following many of the rules of colour harmony might be a recipe for dullness. Quoting the composer Arnold Schoenberg, he noted that harmony is only one of the criteria of musical composition. 'If musical harmony were concerned only with the rules of what sounds well together, it would be limited to a kind of aesthetic etiquette. Instead of telling the musician by what means he can express what, it would teach him only how to behave.'[60]

# IMPRESSIONS AND EXPRESSIONS

Painters have always acknowledged the problems of painting light, but as an aspect of objects and their backgrounds. For Turner, after about 1820, luminosity and atmosphere became an obsession that began to dominate his paintings until, in the later years of his life, pictorial subjects seemed to dissolve into light and colour. Although rooted in the Romantic tradition of ideal landscapes peopled with images from antiquity depicted in sombre and melancholy colours, he progressed towards a fresh and original view of nature and natural forces, expressed by natural harmonies of colour. His palette changed to one of clear brilliant colours, anticipating many of the prescriptions of Goethe's *Zur Farbenlehre* ('Theory of Colours'; 1810), which came into his hands in translation only in 1843.[61] The theory is almost precisely illustrated by one of Turner's favourites among his own paintings, *The Fighting Temeraire* (1838; National Gallery, London). A hazy area, which appears yellow with the light behind it, turns progressively orange, red and finally black as the light intensifies. The colour structure of this painting could be interpreted as an illustration for Goethe's description of the blue-yellow polarity in the sun, the clouds, the smoke and the blue sky.[62]

## The Impressionists

Some fifty years later, the informal group of painters known as the Impressionists devoted their attention to the difficulties of capturing the colours of the changing light and shadows associated with people and objects. Claude Monet was concerned in particular with the latter. Figures almost disappeared from his paintings; he stopped travelling and began to concentrate on series of paintings of natural objects and buildings: poplars, haystacks, Rouen Cathedral and the Gare St Lazare in Paris. The rural subjects are lacking in topographical interest, and the paintings of buildings tell us little about the architecture. He had become absorbed, as Turner had more than half a century before, by the transient effects of light and colour to such an extent that the subject of any given scene had ceased to have any importance.

For me a landscape does not exist in its own right, since its appearance changes at every moment; but the surrounding atmosphere brings it to life — the air and the light which vary continually. For me, it is only the surrounding atmosphere which gives subjects their true value.[63]

But it was not only the bright illuminated effects that attracted him. Of London he wrote: 'I like London only in the winter: without the fog, London would not be a beautiful city. It is the fog which gives it its marvellous breadth. Its regular massive blocks become grandiose in this mysterious cloak.'[64]

Looking back at these extraordinarily creative developments in the history of painting, it is possible to see them as stages in the explorations of light and colour, time and movement, which led ultimately to the new medium of moving pictures. Painters turned away from the representation of nature as the primary purpose of art, focusing instead on the direct expression of feelings and emotions through line, form and colour. In 1908 Henri Matisse wrote:

> What I am after above all is expression . . . The chief aim of colour should be to serve expression as well as possible. To paint an autumn landscape I will try to remember what colour suits the season; I will be inspired only by the sensation the season gives me.[65]

*Colour Expression*

Expressionist groups had appeared almost simultaneously in France and Germany, the Fauves having combined in their art the theories of Vincent van Gogh and Paul Gauguin and retained a certain harmony of design. The group known as Die Brücke used form and colour to express drama and violence: 'We accept all the colours, which, directly or indirectly reproduce the pure creative impulse.' (Ludwig Kirchner, 1913)[66]

This was no longer the atmospheric colour of Turner and Monet but strong highly saturated colour imbued with meaning; and, as with most German art, the meaning was weighted with philosophical concepts. The process by which colours and forms themselves became the repositories of the pictorial idea was carried to its logical conclusion in abstraction.[67]

Attempts to reconcile the more anarchic impulses of Expressionism with the need for social reform were realised in the ideas of the Activist movement, in particular, in the architecture of Bruno Taut (see below) and in the principles on which the Bauhaus (1919-33) was founded.

*ABOVE: The Rietveld-Schröder House (1924) by Gerrit Rietveld. With remarkable restraint strong saturated colours were restricted to linear and structural elements — a lesson that might have been learnt from nature. Volumes resolve themselves into subtly coloured advancing and receding planes, which seduce the eye with the elegance of their proportions*

## The Bauhaus and De Stijl

The importance of colour in the Bauhaus was ensured by the appointment of many artists and designers who had been connected with the Expressionist movement in painting. The links between form, space and colour were confirmed by the foundation course, 'Colour and Form' taught by Johannes Itten, Paul Klee and Wassily Kandinsky and later by Josef Albers, who was at first a student. Each had a different approach, which was reflected in their subsequent development. Itten and Kandinsky believed in a correlation between emotional states, colours and forms; Kandinsky, who had derived his colour theories from Goethe via the anthroposophist Rudolf Steiner, had in 1912 published a paper entitled *Concerning the Spiritual in Art*.[68] From an early age he had experienced synaesthesia (a condition in which sensory impressions overlap, the most common being the association of colours with sounds); he wanted colours to exist purely for their own sake, as sounds do. Paul Klee, an accomplished violinist as well as an artist, considered that the 'pitch' of colours functioned like major or minor keys, enabling a person to 'improvise freely on the chromatic keyboard'.[69] Characteristically, drawing was for Klee 'taking a line for a walk' and changing its character according to what happened on the way. He saw colour as the richest aspect of optical experience: 'while line is only measurement, tone is measurement and weight, colour is quality.'[70]

Although the influence of the Bauhaus on all areas of design has been profound, it did not immediately stimulate the application of colour to the outsides of buildings. White was — and remains in the common perception — the colour associated with the Modern Movement in architecture. Apart from the elaborate and extensive use of applied colour in the social projects of Bruno Taut, it was limited to a few individual projects, among them the Rietveld-Schröder House (1924) by Gerrit Rietveld and the terrace of houses in Pessac (c1926) by Pierre Jeanneret and Le Corbusier.

As an icon of the De Stijl movement, the Rietveld-Schröder House must be seen as exceptional, divorced as it is from the surroundings of its suburban street in Utrecht. The purity of line, form and surface speak of a time when painters, sculptors and architects could work together to such an extent that their work seems interchangeable. With remarkable restraint, strong saturated colours were restricted to linear and structural elements — a lesson that might have been learned from nature. Volume resolves itself into subtly coloured advancing and receding planes that seduce the eye with the elegance of their proportions, reminding

*ABOVE AND NEXT PAGE: Housing in Peterlee new town, Co Durham, England.*
*Peterlee is unique among the British new towns in projecting a specific colour image. This is the result of the employment of the painter Victor Pasmore who worked as a consultant to the chief architect ATW Marsden from 1954 to 1967. The commission was prompted by dissatisfaction with the dull impression created by some of the housing that had been built on traditional lines on the plateau to the north of the centre. Pasmore had the advantage of being able to see buildings more in terms of forms and surfaces expressing colour than as combinations of materials enclosing space. In particular, he realised that the local traditional red brick, which worked well in terms of small groups of farm buildings, became oppressive when used over large areas in contrast to the bright green of the grass. Accordingly, he changed the basic brick colour from red to neutral brownish greys, flattened the roofs and incorporated carefully co-ordinated wooden panels of dark red, brown, beige and yellow ochre with white, which he used also as a framing colour*

us that De Stijl is much more suited to buildings than to chairs.

Memories of De Stijl — particularly of the geometry, proportions and use of colour in the Rietveld-Schröder House — re-emerged in a different form and period with the post-war housing built for the British new town of Peterlee by Victor Pasmore (see Colour Perception).

### Bruno Taut (1880-1938)

As a young man in his twenties Bruno Taut was torn between painting and architecture. In his diary he wrote:

> . . . thoughts about painting occupy me constantly. It seems that I can give my character its fullest expression in this medium — probably better than in architecture . . . The idea that I have already carried around with me for two years still occupies me — the combination of my talents with regard to colour with my architectural ability. Spatial composition with colour, coloured architecture — these are areas in which I shall perhaps say something special . . . [71]

The first opportunity to combine the rational and social skills of the architect with the vision of the painter came in 1914, when he was commissioned to design the small garden suburb of Falkenberg, near Grunau in eastern Berlin. The colours selected were 'light red, dull olive green, golden brown and a strong [intense or highly saturated] blue, and white'. Contemporary observers interpreted the use of colours as a form of liberation, 'freeing working-men's housing from the tyranny of refined and alien forms'. Taut saw it in terms of 'liberating architecture from the straitjacket of muddy grey styles'.[72]

He expressed similar views when he won a place on the Board of Works of the industrial city of Magdeburg in March 1921. The city had degenerated into a dull grey suburb of Berlin and badly needed rejuvenation. Taut proposed to transform it into a colourful city using unbroken colour (unmodified strong colours), beginning with Breiterweg, the main business street. Although he succeeded in his plans for painting a number of public buildings, where the shopkeepers were involved the experiment was a failure. The air was too dirty, the cement render crumbling and the paint of poor quality. The result, after little less than a year, was a disaster, and he resigned.

Subsequent projects for which Taut did not have to rely upon direct public co-operation were more rewarding. As artistic director of the planning division of GEHAG (the public housing board), he became involved in building a number of estates, subsidised by foreign capital,

*PREVIOUS PAGE, ABOVE L AND R: Falkenberg (1914) near Grunau, Berlin, by Bruno Taut.*
*The small garden estate of workers' houses at Falkenberg was dubbed 'the paintbox colony' because of the bold use of colour. Contemporary observers saw its use as a form of liberation, freeing working-men's housing from the tyranny of 'refined and alien forms'. Situated in the former East Berlin, it carries a plaque celebrating Taut's contribution to society before he was compelled to leave the country because of the rise of the Nazi regime*

*PREVIOUS PAGE, BELOW L: Bruno Taut's bold and surprising bands of red and blue on white offered an interesting solution to the problem of giving identity to these large-scale housing blocks (1927-28) at Prenzlauer Berg, Weissensee, Berlin*

*PREVIOUS PAGE, BELOW R: The main horseshoe-shaped central block of Taut's Hufeisensiedlung (1925-27), Berlin, carries little colour other than white, the strong reds, yellows and the occasional blue being limited to the smaller terraces of houses outside*

throughout the city of Berlin and had more freedom to implement his ideas of colour. The buildings included a long multi-storey slab block of low-cost flats at the Prenzlauer Berg in the Weissensee district; this was boldly painted with broad bands of red and blue against white and was an interesting early solution to the problem of giving identity to large-scale housing blocks by means of colour. There were also two other large estate developments known as the Hufeisensiedlung (1922-27), named after the horseshoe-shaped central block, and the Waldsiedlung ('woodland estate') Zehlendorf (1926-32), nicknamed 'Onkel Toms Hütte' ('Uncle Tom's Cabin').

For the last of the five phases of the Waldsiedlung Zehlendorf, the building authorities required a unified colour scheme to be submitted in advance for approval. Five parallel streets of two-storey houses were painted in 'Pompeian red' and bluish green, alternating left and right, the complementary scheme being reversed on the backs of the houses. The facades were articulated with bands of glazed brick in the manner of Piet Mondrian, with dividing walls of natural red brick, and the window frames were carefully articulated in black and white, red and yellow. The use of the complementary red and green reflected the natural light conditions, the west-facing facades being red and the east-facing walls green. The colours of the window frames depended on the particular background wall colour in each case; the ends of the streets were 'closed' with strategically coloured blocks. Taut described the colour choices in spatial terms:

> . . . colour should be used to underline the spatial character of the development. By means of variation in colour intensity and brilliance we can expand the space between the houserows in certain directions and compress it in others. Thus one of the key principles behind the colour scheme is an optical widening of both streets and yards by means of relatively dark colours. This also has the emotional advantage that on the garden side of the houses, the glass-roofed verandas will appear lighter against the unbroken walls above them if these walls are rendered a darker blue . . . [73]

The fact that the applied colours survived on the houses of all these estates is a measure of Bruno Taut's success. They have degenerated in the sense that the weather has washed and bleached the paints and early repainting was not co-ordinated, but this degeneration can be seen as an aspect of human evolution, particularly apparent now that restorations have been undertaken. It is becoming clear that some degree of flexibility is desirable within a planning framework for colour.

*OPPOSITE AND LEFT: Onkel Toms Hütte (Uncle Tom's Cabin; 1926-32), Waldsiedlung, Zehlendorf.*
*This is in many ways the most outstanding of the four estates in Berlin by Bruno Taut. It is spatially well organised, displaying a sensitivity to the shape of the site and the relationships of buildings to pines and birch trees, all of which are enhanced by the use of colour. These effects are to some extent a result of Taut's work (in conjunction with the two other architects Haring and Salvisberg) on the first phase of the development south of the railway and the main road, the Argentinische Allee, which can be seen as experimental. For the last of the five phases of the development (Waldsiedlung Zehlendorf), the building authorities required a unified colour scheme to be submitted in advance for approval. The colour scheme was based on the principle of using the complementary red and green on opposite sides of the five parallel streets of three-storey houses as a reflection of natural lighting, the west-facing facades being red and those facing east being green. The house fronts are separated by dividing walls of natural red brick. Strong (highly saturated) colour is confined to the windows and doors. The former have a three-way colour scheme of black/white/black and red/black/red alternating between houses, with yellow/black/yellow; on the window frames of the 'lost' (recessed) third storey. The front doors are plain white. On the back facades where the walls are green, the windows are red/yellow/red with yellow/black/yellow in the white part of the upper storey*

But the message is clear, as Taut wrote in 1925:

> Everything in the world has colour of some sort. Nature has colour — even the grey of dust and soot, even gloom has colour of some kind. Where there is light there must be colour. All man has to do is to give this phenomenon form . . . as soon as he does this, he bathes the drabness in the rays of the sun. Since everything has colour, everything that people do must have colour.[74]

### Le Corbusier (1887-1965)

The painter-architect Le Corbusier wanted to do something poetic with the houses at Pessac. He embraced colour completely, seeking to achieve an effect of weightlessness by painting the surfaces in different colours that met at the corners, so that a light grey, for example, bordered on a light sky-blue without any hint of structural thickness. Rasmussen described his experience of sitting in the shade of a maple tree in the roof garden of one of the houses:

> I could see how the sun dappled the Havana-brown wall with blobs of light. The only purpose of the wall was to frame the view. The buildings opposite could be perceived as houses only with great difficulty. The one to the left was simply a light green plane without cornice or gutter. An oblong hole was cut out of the plane exactly like the one I was looking through. Behind and to the right of the green house were row-houses with coffee-brown facades and cream-coloured sides and behind them rose the tops of blue 'sky-scrapers' [penthouses].[75]

The subsequent development of Le Corbusier's architecture and planning, and the public disillusion with Modernism, have over-shadowed his continuing involvement in painting. He loved what he called 'the powerful hum of colour', using it as an important feature of most of his buildings. Significantly, the house he designed for the Weissenhofsiedlung — the showcase for modern architecture in Stuttgart — is virtually the only one with any external colour, and the colour of the window reveals was an important feature of the Unité d'Habitation in Marseilles (1947-52) and later buildings in Chandigarh (1950-56).

*OPPOSITE, ABOVE AND BELOW: Supreme Court, Chandigarh, India, 1950-56, by Le Corbusier. Colour remained an important feature of Le Corbusier's buildings, although he never again used it as whole-heartedly as in the transformation of his terrace housing at Pessac, Bordeaux (1922-26)*

# COLOUR EFFECTS

Although it is possible to measure light waves and their colour frequencies by electronic means, this does not solve the problem of understanding and using colour in the environment. The difficulty is threefold: first in understanding the relationships between light and pigment (see The Nature of Colour); second in coping with the three variable colour 'dimensions' (see In Search of Harmony); and third, in coming to terms with the physical and sensory aspects of its use, which are discussed in this chapter.

Size and shape, angle and alignment are important not only in the two-dimensional 'pictorial' sense, but in the proportional relationships between adjacent coloured surfaces, since colour is fundamentally about relationships, which change according to different juxtapositions. In addition, colours seem to move, to advance and retreat, to spread and contract. Some colours are hot and some are cold. Some appear heavy, others light. There are, moreover, many intractable ways in which colours affect our emotional state. As neurologists explore further into the cerebral sites of our senses, explanations may be found, as Herbert Read suggests:

> The range of colours . . . might be placed to correspond with our emotions; red corresponding with anger, yellow with joy, blue with longing and so on. There is probably a simple physiological explanation for this correspondence, the pleasure or discomfort [caused] by the frequency with which the waves or rays of light strike the retina of the eye . . . [76]

*Size and Proportion*
Judgements of harmony between small 'captive' areas of colour in a similar format are quite different from those in the field, which involve enormous differences in size, much more subtle and complex combinations of colours and the effects of constantly changing light. The addition of scale as a fourth 'dimension' to any system of harmony would make it unworkable, but it is a vital factor, acknowledged by both Ostwald and Munsell, who recommend that highly saturated colours should be

confined to small surfaces and that the colours of large surfaces should be relatively subdued.[77] As a principle of nature, it cannot be faulted.

The size of a colour surface is important because of its relative dominance. If it is too large it can be monotonous or overpowering; if too small, it can be lost. The 'bulking' or massing effect of large buildings in the landscape is well known, and various kinds of camouflage have been applied, including the visual 'targeting' of particular units or buildings by using geometric and other patterns (see The Purpose of Colour and below). These work well in large controlled developments such as power and military installations, but they are more difficult to apply in urban situations where buildings are often jostling for attention.

The problem varies according to the situation, the proximity of the coloured surfaces to the observer and the relative local colour of the surfaces. Goethe proposed simple ratios between colours, to which he gave numerical values, as follows: yellow 9, orange 8, red 6, violet 3, blue 4 and green 6. The resultant ratios for pairs of complementary colours were thus yellow:violet 3:1, orange:blue 2:1 and red:green 1:1. While the interpretation of these ratios is dependent on circumstances, they are a useful starting point for considering how colours might be balanced. We know, for instance, that yellow generally reflects more light than red and that red is more intense than blue under conditions of normal daylight, although the visibility of red and blue is reversed as the light fades. The test, perhaps, is to accommodate such changes in the design and application of colours. The paintings of Piet Mondrian and Ben Nicholson are valuable references because of the extreme care that they took to balance sizes, shapes and colours, but there is a world of difference between the controlled environment of the art gallery or studio and that of the world outside.

We see and balance objects and their colours against one another and their backgrounds. This becomes such an automatic activity that it is usually unselfconscious; it is also mainly personal or private. It becomes self-conscious when we lay the table, furnish a room or decorate the house; outside it becomes public. There is an important visual and colour relationship between the lock and the door, between the door and the porch and the surrounding wall, between these and the ones next door and so on along the street (see Colour Control).

### Shapes and Patterns of Colour

The horizontal and vertical alignments that have exerted a greater hold on our perceptions since the expansion of technology are reinforced by

*ABOVE: West India Dock.*
*The narrow bands of strong highly saturated colour serve to emphasise the form and character of this sports building in London Docklands as well as expressing the divisions according to the precepts of Rasmussen. The orange band simulates a cornice, so often lacking in industrial sheds*

colour (see High Colour). Small variations that occur in lettering, signs and logos may be acceptable, but dramatic deviations from the geometric norm are disturbing to our sense of equanimity. This may be intended by advertisers, to 'catch the eye', but in the more permanent field of architecture it is questionable. It may be legitimate for artists and designers to reflect the chaos of society, but it is not necessary for them to emphasise it.[78]

Direction plays an important part in the use of colour in signs, adding a useful dynamism in the case of arrows and diagonal warning flashes, for example on the tailboards of lorries, but the use of such devices for the decoration of buildings is likely to be disruptive. The use of stripes of contrasting colours creates a flicker effect, in which the eye moves rapidly from one stripe to another, adapting to the colours by dilation as it does so. This sets up a rhythm that cannot be fulfilled by the colour patterns either of the building itself or of those adjoining. It is akin to the effect experienced when passing fences. The use of such devices in Op Art and in the later colour compositions of Bridget Riley is intriguing, but on the surfaces of buildings it tends to be disturbing, setting aside the few examples of camouflage applied to ships and buildings with care and deliberation (see The Purpose of Colour). An extension of the principle of the flicker effect occurs also in chequerboard patterns. These have been employed frequently in high-rise blocks of flats, where they seemed to suit the juxtapositions of the solids and voids of balconies and walls, but the repeat of the unsatisfying rhythm in both directions is doubly unsatisfying.

*Target and Background*

In terms of the psychology of perception, the 'target–background' or 'figure–ground' relationship is often illustrated by a puzzle. This comprises a drawing of two objects or figures of equal proportions but contrasting colours, which can be read in two different ways. A chequerboard illustrates the problem. When the contrast is removed, the visual problem disappears. Similarly, when looking at an object or building we are confused by dualities and ambiguities (see In Search of Harmony) of shape, form and colour. We expect the 'target' or 'figure' to be clearly defined in contrast with the background, which is generally less well defined, larger and more continuous; this is the norm by which we can orientate ourselves. More precise references to the verticals and horizontals that assist us in keeping our balance and moving on prescribed paths have been described by JJ Gibson as 'ecological

*ABOVE: Warwick University (architects: Renton, Howard, Wood and Levine).*
*Traditional roofs tend to appear darker than the walls, a principle that has been followed in this arts centre building with unusual ingenuity. The bulk is effectively reduced by division into narrow bands, which are faceted to set up a dual rhythm between the bands of closely related (analogous) and highly saturated colours and the light and shade*

optics'.[79] Buildings have undoubtedly become important in our built environment for similar reasons. In simplistic terms, the bright red and yellow lines of the Rietveld-Schröder House, seen close at close quarters, read as targets or figures against the whitish background, in a similar way to the bright touches of colour in nature. From a distance, only the white would be seen (see Colour Guidelines). If the colour areas were transposed, the reverse would be true. Such contraventions of the natural order need justification.

In a general survey of traditional farm buildings in Britain, AC Hardy (see Colour Guidelines) found that walls generally contrasted with the surrounding landscape and that roofs were generally darker than the walls.[80] Similar conclusions might also be drawn from studies of building traditions in most countries, which could provide a basis for general development in both town and country. Many authorities would consider that such a rule-of-thumb approach is already practised, even if it has not been formulated. The 'surface colours' of walls and roofs are predominant and should therefore be carefully related to their background; they are punctuated by doors, windows and their frames and by such details as bargeboards, cornices, gutters and downpipes, each of which has colour. All these colours are considered in the method pioneered by Jean-Philippe Lenclos (see Colour and Place); colours are related back to their origins, whether natural or synthetic, and the buildings to their regions, to provide a sound basis for colour design; he describes it as the 'geography of colour'.[81]

## Colour Temperature, Weight and Movement

Red is hot and blue is cold. We speak of things as being 'red hot', undoubtedly associating the image with fire and blood and perhaps anger and love. Yellow is warm, sunny and joyful, in contrast with blue, which is cool and contemplative. We can arrange these hues in their most saturated form, according to their relative temperatures. Yet the effects of these colours can be changed if we modify them. We can make a warm blue, a cooler red and a cold bitter yellow by mixing colours. Such changes can be achieved by Pointillist and layering techniques, which exaggerate the colour change, for example, from a reddish blue at midday to a bluish red in the evening (see The Purpose of Colour).

The term 'weight' was adopted by the British Standards Institute (BS 5252) with 'greyness' to describe more precisely the differences between paint colours. While greyness expresses the practical difference

*OVERLEAF, ABOVE L: We expect the 'figure' or object to be clearly defined and in contrast with the background, which is generally less well defined, larger and more continuous. In this view in Snape, Suffolk, the eye is seduced and the picture dominated by basic contrasts, simple geometry and unexpected colour relationships. The square white door seen against the black background dominates the view and distracts from the miscellany of other buildings, which by virtue of their colours are visually attached to the background, a phenomenon common in camouflage*

*OVERLEAF, ABOVE R: The hut at the head of the water supply pipe was probably painted green to blend with the Snowdonian landscape — which it fails to do for three reasons: its geometric shape, its smooth surface and the blue-green colour. The latter, particularly, has a disturbingly ambiguous relationship with the complex colours of the landscape: a degree of contrast using red, brown, black or even a carefully chosen yellow would have been preferable*

*OVERLEAF, BELOW L: In this view of the Ronchamps Chapel by Le Corbusier the eye is first seduced by the white wall, second by the white and yellow triangles and third by the fairly neutral purple and the receding blue. One might ask, 'What does it mean?'*

*OVERLEAF, BELOW R: The 'figure' or visual target is multiplied in a progression of similar colours and shapes in this view of suburban houses in Petworth. They follow certain principles: being sited against a dark background, having roofs darker than their walls and the colours of both blending in unusual analogous harmony with the soil colours of the arable landscape, with which they have a rhythmical relationship. The harmony will become one of opposites when the field becomes green*

in apparent grey content between one colour and another, weight is a modification of value, referring to lightness or darkness.[82] This is equivalent or at least similar to the notional idea that some colours look heavier than others. It is graphically illustrated by sequences of a single hue graduated from the lightest at the top to the darkest at the bottom.

Colour can be used to express movement in a number of different ways. This may be implicit in the nature of the colour itself, in eye movements caused by the juxtaposition of colours or by actual movement of coloured materials or lights. Aerial perspective — the use of blue to suggest distance, long employed by painters and used occasionally on buildings (see Colour and Space) — is an obvious example of the first. The eye is led by any directional use of colour and by graduated sequences, but most dramatically by the use of the flicker effect described above. The physical movement of coloured elements has been developed ingeniously as electronically controlled sun-screening for the Thamesside office of Richard Rogers.[83]

ABOVE: A Pointillist technique has been used on this building near Stuttgart, combining red and blue to mix optically into purple when seen from a distance, the relative predominance of each of the two colours depending on the time of day, as explained by the Purkinje Shift (colour design: Gottfried Prölss)

L, ABOVE: Target and background. The red brick building and tennis court merge into one area of colour at a distance. The sense of ambiguity becomes overwhelming when the distinction between the relative proportions of 'figure' and 'ground' and of their colours is unclear. The effect can be claustrophobic: a reason perhaps why the red material of this playground at Sheen School, London, has been replaced

L, BELOW: Two types of white are visible in this scene near Berwick. The brilliant white forms a visual target that attracts the eye, while the ordinary white is much less obtrusive

# COLOUR AND SPACE

Our experiences of colour and space are at once concrete and abstract. Both are in many ways insubstantial. Colour at least can be seen; space can only be described in terms of form — of objects and containment. The Greek philosopher Parmenides maintained that space could not exist because it could not be seen, but Plato introduced the idea of geometry, which was further defined by Aristotle in his theory of place, or *topos*. Space was seen as the sum of all places, a dynamic field with directions and qualitative properties,[84] which can be interpreted as space and character in the landscape. 'Whereas space denotes the three-dimensional organisation of the elements which make up a place, character denotes the general atmosphere which is the most comprehensive property of any place.'[85]

We speak of activities 'taking place'; it is meaningless to imagine occurrences without reference to localities, which might be defined by name, by historical or geographical association or in concrete terms of shape, form, materials and colour.[86] For the most part the focus is on the concrete aspects, since our perceptions are object-oriented, but at the deeper existential level it is the sequence of spaces that directs our movements, and these are influenced by colour. As Klee observed, 'line is only measurement, tone is measurement and weight, but colour is quality'.

Everyone has experience of space. From infancy our movements are spatially oriented: we learn to negotiate objects and people, developing particular skills in sports, dancing and acting, which are structured extensions of the process of understanding space. Yet attempts to understand space by analysis, recording and design present particular difficulties, which have been only partially addressed. These attempts began with the Renaissance, when Italian painters and architects began to impose a rational order on the relatively disordered patterns of the cities; it continued with the movement towards informality. Neither of these approaches gave much consideration to colour. They have been succeeded in the twentieth century first by the rediscovery of vernacular architecture and second by the 'discovery' of colour.

*OPPOSITE, ABOVE: Most of the traditional colours on the island of Bornholm are either white or in the red–yellow range. The pale blue on the wall at the end of the street in the fishing village of Gudjheim serves to exaggerate the distance*

*OPPOSITE, BELOW: In Britain colours tend to be muted, heavily reliant upon the traditional black and white, but with occasional enhancements, as here in a village in the valley of the River Darenth in Kent, England*

*OPPOSITE, R: Collioure. The blue and green shuttered windows watch like bright eyes in this Mediterranean painters' town in the Roussillon region, eastern Pyrenees*

*OPPOSITE, L AND ABOVE: Orange, France. Some of the most beautiful effects are achieved by the simplest means, using few colours and relying on reflected light, as in this narrow street; The self-conscious use of colour has made the main town square 'colourful' with too many different colours*

*BELOW: Tournus, France. In most places colour appearance depends upon a mixture of material colours and those applied in the form of paint*

Fixed-point perspective was an invention of the artists of the Italian Renaissance to represent a three-dimensional view on a flat plane, thereby capturing space and distance. The principle was embodied in the new Renaissance cities with their straight streets, unbroken roof lines, round arches and repetition of such uniform elements as cornices, windows, lintels and the columns of the facades.[87] Together they came to express what Lewis Mumford calls 'the ideology of power', using geometry to organise space and 'make it continuous, reduce it to measure and order, and to extend the limits of magnitude, embracing the extremely distant and the extremely minute: finally to associate space with motion and time.'[88]

The new order was popular and throughout the world has remained symbolic of authority, contrasted almost everywhere with more organic and perhaps more chaotic systems of urban form and space, which Christopher Alexander describes as the self-conscious and the unself-conscious (see Colour and Place). In Britain where many symbols of formality were adopted, there was a long-standing reaction against this, which found an outlet in the park-like gardens of Lancelot 'Capability' Brown. They were inspired by the serpentine 'Line of Beauty' described by the painter William Hogarth, which Brown expressed by means of an undulating surface and of serpentine lines on the ground, thus expressing a harmony between the movements of people and the designed 'natural' landscape. The experience is described by Edmund Burke (1767):

> Most people have observed the sort of sense they have had of being swiftly drawn in an easy coach on a smooth turf, with gradual ascents and declivities. This will give a better idea of the Beautiful than almost anything else.[89]

The spatial experience was typically recorded in literature and landscape rather than in drawings, in which both the curvature and the corresponding sense of movement were problematical. There are interesting parallels both in the 'ecological optics' of JJ Gibson[90] and in the 'travelling eye' convention of Chinese painting. EH Gombrich describes the experience of the former:

> Walking or riding towards an object on ground level and fixing our eyes on it, we see it not only increase in size but we also perceive 'a panoramic flow' of the surround which opens up before us and swings round in a regular pattern. In this situation the asymmetry of the flow will either denote that we have swayed from our course and must adjust it, or that the ground is not level.[91]

The Chinese convention of the 'travelling eye' was a method of representing three dimensions in one plane by the use of many viewpoints at different levels, a process involving the spectator in both time and space. It reached the height of its expression in scroll painting of the Shen Kua period (eleventh century AD). There are many parallels in the work of Paul Cézanne, the Cubists and, later, David Hockney.[92]

The changing experiences as the body moves, and with it the viewpoint of the eye, are referred to by Gordon Cullen as 'serial vision'. In order to take account of this phenomenon, the artist or architect must record both the existing view and the emerging view by means of photographs and sketches in 'the art of relationship': 'One building standing alone in the countryside is experienced as a work of architecture; bring half a dozen buildings together and an art other than architecture is made possible . . .'[93] Cullen used the word 'townscape' to describe the collection of urban 'buildings, trees, nature, water, traffic, advertisements . . .' that make the city 'a dramatic event in the environment'. Such words as progression, rhythm, punctuation, intimacy, enclosure, entanglement and surprise are used by him in reference to places with individual qualities of 'colour, texture, scale, style, character, personality, uniqueness'.[94] The principles were precisely in tune with the growing conservation movement in Britain. It suddenly became clear why old towns are so special, and Cullen's work led the way to improving them — although he was to regret the many superficial interpretations of his principles in the form of cobbles and bollards. The expression 'of townscape value' has since become common usage in planning.

Although colour was implied as an aspect of materials in the early seventies, it was not regarded as a major element of planning, perhaps because of the architectural inhibitions of the time. There has since been an explosion of colour almost everywhere — occasionally part of a planned strategy and sometimes brilliant in its composition, but more often lacking co-ordination and meaning. Yet the scope is enormous and the possibilities are endless, for colour is readily available, easily mixable and inexpensive and is thus eminently suited to a new interpretation of space. Patrick Heron draws on the analogy of painting:

Because painting is concerned with the *seen*, as distinct from the *known*, pictorial space and pictorial colour are virtually synonymous . . . for the human eye there is no space without its colour; and no colour that does not create its own space. When you open your eyes the texture of the entire visual field consists of one thing: and that is colour . . . [95]

# COLOUR AND PLACE

Although it is clear that colour is a significant aspect of every place, explanations of its particular role are beset with difficulties. The colour of the landscape is responsible for such names as Colorado, the Redlands, Rothenburg and Collonges-la-Rouge, and associations between colours and places are recorded in such names as Red Square, Venetian red and Turin yellow (see Colour Planning). Moreover, surprising numbers of variations on just a few colour themes are found when towns and villages of different countries and regions — even different districts of the same town or city — are compared. In considering what conclusions can be drawn from these factors it is necessary to ask whether they represent only the remnants of a dying culture or whether, as is to be hoped, they can be used as a means of informing the present and planning the future.

*Colour Precedents*
As a visual medium, colour depends upon precedents that can be judged visually. The most obvious of these are the old towns and villages that are often described as 'colourful' — mostly places with large numbers of painted buildings, for example, such as Burano (Italy), Schärding (Austria), Szentendre (Hungary) and Guanajuato (Mexico). To these must be added those other traditional places distinguished by the uses and colours of natural materials and also the many examples in which the natural colours and those of paint are combined. Most places combine the two to a large extent; Venice, Rome, Florence and Bologna, for example, conjure up images of colour without clear recollections of the precise nature of their materials. This is one of the difficulties of colour analysis. Yet analysis also reveals the evidence of successive historical cultures, identifying new objects and buildings, colours and even colour traditions (see below) that might be considered intrusive, disturbing the integrity of the place. This applies in all locations, whether or not they have been designated as conservation areas. However, such designations are valuable as a starting point, since they are almost always made on a historical basis in cities and can thus provide the foun-

dation for a suitable approach.

Paintings are an additional source of visual evidence, for two reasons. More importantly, they provide a kind of visual laboratory for learning about colour relationships and their effects. They also offer social and topographic insights into the life of the past, although historical illustrations of painted streets should not be taken too literally. Even if it could be demonstrated that the artists' colours were an accurate representation of the colour washes used on walls and their correct sequence (a record of fact rather than the exercise of artistic licence), the picture could only be regarded as depicting a particular moment in history when all the houses were newly painted, rather than the generality of historical continuity. For traditions essentially represent periods of development in the process of history. Although this process is continuous, embracing past, present and future, it has been interrupted by a variety of changes, of which the growth of industry and the consequent transfer of human responsibilities from individuals to larger organisations are major examples. These changes, which cannot be dated historically with any degree of precision because they have occurred at different times in different places, underlie the transition from the 'unselfconscious' to the 'self-conscious' process of making and designing, discussed by Christopher Alexander (see below). It began with the Renaissance and the growth of rationalism (the reliance on human intellect) but it has been long and slow in its effect and was first recognised by a few individuals in the nineteenth century, being accepted by the majority only at the close of the twentieth. It is easy to be sentimental about it, seeking to retain or revive lost cultures, but it is more important to consider reasonably what has been lost and what gained. The decline of crafts and craftsmanship has been accompanied by the growth of design and designers of all kinds.

*Unselfconscious and Self-conscious Processes*

Christopher Alexander distinguishes between the unselfconscious and self-conscious processes of making colour decisions with reference to the following anecdote.[96] There was a long tradition of shawl-making among peasants working in family groups in parts of Slovakia. The shawls were wonderfully patterned and coloured using vegetable dyes. When synthetic aniline dyes were introduced early in the twentieth century, however, many of the shawls became vulgar and uninteresting. The reason was not so much the quality as the variety of the colours: there were too many. The shawl-makers were not artists but

*OPPOSITE, FROM ABOVE L TO R: Red and yellow in architecture, exemplified by Guanajuato, Mexico; Szentendre, Hungary; Rønne, Bornholm; Barnes, London; Heron Quays, London Docklands; Byker, Newcastle.*
*No colour is as territorial as red. Venetian painters used red from oxide of iron for a warm ground, and red lead was used for protecting iron and steel. Red advances and contracts. Close up in daylight it dominates, especially when highly saturated, and is difficult to handle unless mixed or relieved by lighter colours such as yellow or white.*
*Yellow is the most reflective of colours after the achromatic white and is the most easily seen — one reason why it is used for lifebelts and rescue craft, road markings and signs. Like red it appears to advance, but unlike red it spreads. Among the hues it is brightest when fully saturated, whereas the others become darker; when yellow darkens it ceases to appear yellow. Pure yellow occurs only in a narrow band of the spectrum compared with the other primary colours. In nature, yellow occurs commonly in the minerals sulphur, gold and orpiment — a sulphide of arsenic and an important pigment in the ancient world. It is also, with red, orange, brown, pink and purple, produced by the iron compounds common almost everywhere in geology. In its lighter versions yellow is commonly used in building, but when it is highly saturated it needs calming with white*

craftspeople able to make well-considered judgements only within the limitations of their craft and its range of available colours. Once they were presented with more complicated choices, their apparent mastery and judgement deserted them. Likewise, in most human endeavours this unselfconscious process has now been supplanted by self-conscious processes — by rationalism and design.

There is a direct parallel in the design and decoration of houses, in the breakdown of traditions and the spread of a pluralistic approach, which may be welcomed or deplored. The intensive production of aniline dyes and paints, which began in the 1860s, has undoubtedly had a dramatic effect on advertising and on the commercial development of cities, as well as on the colouring of high-rise housing developments. On the other hand, the effect upon individual houses has been limited. Whether this is owing to an innate conservatism and sense of appropriateness connected with the place can only be a matter of speculation, but if this is indeed the case it might imply some deep sense of ecological propriety that derives from our adaptive predispositions in relation to locations and their natural features, building materials and history (see The Purpose of Colour). Reducing the problem of colour and place to simplistic terms, we may think of the place drawn as a plan in two dimensions showing locations and directions. If we extend it upwards in three dimensions it describes the space; then colour can be visualised as the fourth dimension.

*Colour Traditions*

Colour traditions apply to both material and applied colours — those that are innate and those painted on the surface. In reality both occur together and the latter often derive from the former. This is evident in some of the colours commonly used for painting the rendered surfaces of neoclassical buildings, and it has been suggested that the frequent use of red and yellow on houses in Scandinavia was originally in imitation of the brick and stone colours of 'grand' houses.[97] The practical reasons for the uses of paint and the choices of colour are many and various. Availability and cost have always been important considerations, and the basic colours — black, white and a range of colours in the yellow, red and brown spectrum — are almost universally available. Protection of porous materials is a significant factor that has given rise to the use of render of various kinds, including mud and plaster, and to colour-wash traditions all over the world.

Where there is little stone or it is of poor quality there is a need for plaster or render as a binding material, which itself has given rise to colour traditions. The common use of lime for this purpose, both inside and outside houses, was found to be valuable as a hygienic measure, and the islanders of the Cyclades were so much afraid of plague that they carried the white painting out over the paving of the streets. In seventeenth-century Britain lime was also regarded as a useful fire-retardant and frequently painted over all internal and external surfaces, including the thatch of the roof. Such practical uses of a white substance undoubtedly had symbolic value; in England white was associated with good luck and its bearers the white witches, who, it has been suggested, were encouraged to enter houses through white-painted windows.[98] The fact that white reflects and thereby reduces the heat may have contributed to the tradition of white rendering prevalent in towns and villages across the Mediterranean from Portugal to the Turkish coast. Although the cuboid houses are very similar in form, the settlements are distinguished from one another by stylistic and colour differences in important buildings, notably churches, and in the careful and distinctive uses of colour for outlining openings and painting shutters and doors.

The value of these traditions is in their unifying effect and affirmation of local character. Where the villages have become depopulated, as is so often the case, and the buildings are falling into disrepair, this effect has more relevance to the past than to the present. Where they are maintained there are indications of new colour influences — welcome or otherwise — coinciding with the availability of new paint colours. Since it is the nature of traditions to develop and grow, interference with what might be seen as an accurate reflection of developing society is perhaps an intrusion. On the other hand it cannot be denied that society has been disrupted, although the precise nature of the disruption and its timing are difficult to specify.

The translation of traditions from one place to another cannot be prevented any more than it can justifiably be deplored. Technical and stylistic ideas have always travelled, and the same is true of colour traditions. Both the clapboard houses of the eastern USA and the red barns of the mid-west came originally from Europe — the former from England, the latter from Norway and Sweden. Since their arrival in the Scandinavian settlements of the USA, the red barns have spread eastwards, and also westwards as far as the Rocky Mountains. Reasons given for their redness range from symbolic or wood protective functions to the necessity of hiding the rust marks of the nails. The image of

*OPPOSITE, FROM ABOVE L TO R; L, FROM ABOVE:*
*White architecture: The 'functional tradition' of canal-side*
*architecture in England; Chester Terrace, London; the*
*Lizard, Cornwall; Weobley, Herefordshire; Ibiza; Kresge*
*College, California (architects: Charles Moore and*
*William Turnbull); a house in Southern England;*
*the Kremlin, Moscow.*
*Black and white are the two basic colours described in*
*all languages and are among the commonest colours in*
*the environment. 'The first of all simple colours is white,*
*although some would not admit that black and white are*
*colours, the first being a source or receiver of colours,*
*and the latter totally deprived of them. But we cannot*
*leave them out, since painting is but an effect of light*
*and shade, that is chiaroscuro, so white is the first, then*
*yellow, green, blue and red and finally black . . . '*
*(Leonardo da Vinci,* Advice to Artists)
*White is easily obtained from chalk and limestone rocks,*
*from which it was traditionally prepared by mixing the*
*powder with milk or size. It has three great assets: the*
*ability to protect the surface from weather and from heat,*
*cleanliness — in both the hygienic and the psychologi-*
*cal sense — and in its ability to transform visually.*
*When locally grown hardwoods became too scarce and*
*expensive for window frames in late eighteenth-century*
*England, the imported softwood substitutes were often*
*painted in white lead for protection until it was banned*
*on account of being poisonous. Whitewash and white*
*paint are never pure white, nor black pure black: such*
*absolutes are avoided on commercial colour cards. Both*
*take on the reflections of other colours, a fact acknowl-*
*edged by Kasimir Malevich in his painting* White on
White *(1920). White is the perfect foil for any other*
*colour: 'As early as 1910 I knew about the bracing*
*quality of chalk white. Practice showed me that the joy of*
*white explodes only when surrounded by the powerful*
*hum of colour.' (Le Corbusier)*

a white Mediterranean village has been adopted by Charles Moore and William Turnbull for the student hostel at Kresge College in California. Probably the most geologically influenced American tradition — at least in the south-west — is that of the Hispano-Indian buildings of New Mexico, where conscious attempts have been made to conserve the earth colour of the region in the walls and the greenish blue Taos blue (derived from copper) has been used for the timber details. Interesting variations on this Native American tradition have been developed by the architect Antoine Predock in the use of pale local colours simulating colour-wash, for example, in the Hotel Santa Fé that has been built in Euro-Disneyland in France.

Another development is the widespread appearance in towns and cities of colours introduced by immigrant communities. The use of green on houses often indicates inhabitants from Pakistan, green being both the colour of Mohammed's tribal flag and that of the nation. Chinese quarters are distinguished by the use of red, signifying good luck. Indian, Bangladeshi, West Indian and Caribbean communities are all inclined to use combinations of brilliant colours typical of their bright homelands, which easily appear garish in the soft diffused light of northern climates.

### The Geography of Colour

It was in Japan that Jean-Philippe Lenclos first developed the idea of the 'geography of colour'. As a postgraduate student from the Ecole Nationale Supérieure des Arts Décoratifs, Paris, studying in Kyoto, he became aware of the subtleties of natural colours:

> I was suddenly struck by the very special colour sense of Japan, by the extraordinary range of colour in the kimono, by the subtle palette of shades of grey and dark brown in the old wood, and by the enormous variety of colour in ordinary everyday objects.[99]

On his return to France, Lenclos was appointed Artistic Director of the Gauthier Paint Company and charged with the task of developing a range of paint colours suited to the different regions of France. Like Britain, France is rich in regional diversity of landscape, natural materials and colour. The process of industrialisation and the standardisation of materials and techniques — which in Britain was already more advanced — was threatening to make all areas look alike. To counteract this, Lenclos and his colleagues embarked on a long process of study:

> We considered all the information, not subjectively but with scientific detachment. We made sketches of sites, noted materials, col-

*OPPOSITE, FROM ABOVE L TO R: Blue and green architecture: Burano, Italy; Schärding, Austria; Gillingham, Kent; Chippenham, Wiltshire; Romanian village; Jodhpur, India.*

*Blue and green are equivocal colours. They are to some extent interchangeable, the one merging into the other. As the colours of the sky and vegetation they have an ambivalence in their symbolic meanings.*

*Apart from its transient presence in the sky and reflections in water, blue is a colour that is rare in nature — a reason perhaps why blue buildings look self-conscious in the town or country. Although there are many blue flowers, their blues are inclined towards red or purple. The colour occurs in blue eyes, the feathers of some birds, in some insects and fish, but only rarely in animals. The only mineral blues are lapis lazuli, turquoise and azurite. The natural vegetable dyes, indigo and wood, were formerly called 'hidden colours' because of the need for a chemical reaction to reveal them. Ultramarine blue was produced by grinding lapis lazuli. In the Middle Ages it was so rare and precious that its use in painting was limited to the robe of the Virgin Mary. Blue was popular among the Aztecs and Navajo, who associated a blue turquoise with males and a green one with females.*

*Green is ambivalent. It is the colour of life, but it also has negative associations with nausea, poisons and decay. It is the most restful colour to the eye. In daylight, when most of the colour receptor cells are active, they are most sensitive to yellowish green light. There are few green minerals that can be ground as pigments, and no bright green dyes that can be obtained directly from nature. Although common as a detail colour, as a surface colour green is comparatively rare, except in a lightened form and in a few places. In Romania some villages are almost entirely green, but these are among the exceptions. Large areas of saturated green, blue or turquoise have a tendency to appear intrusive among the predominantly warm colours of our built environment*

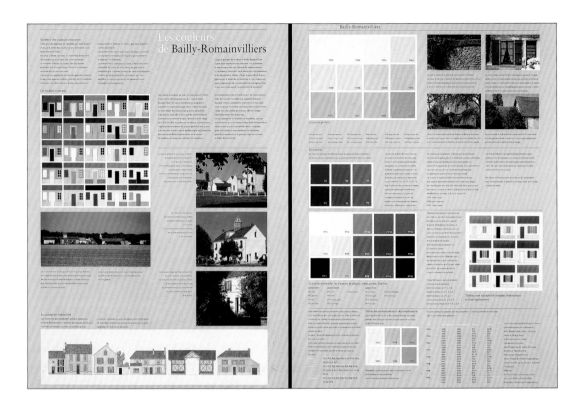

## Les couleurs de Bailly-Romainvilliers

## Les couleurs de Coupvray

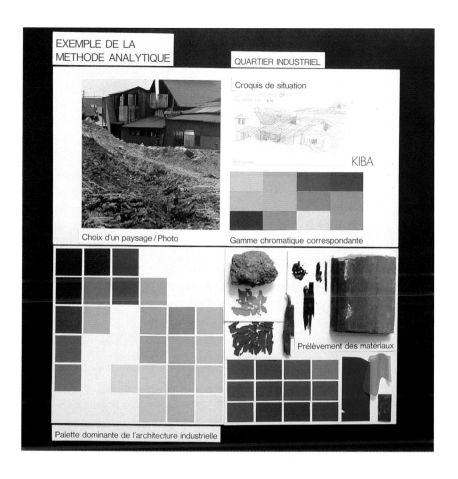

EXEMPLE DE LA METHODE ANALYTIQUE

QUARTIER INDUSTRIEL

Croquis de situation

KIBA

Choix d'un paysage / Photo

Gamme chromatique correspondante

Prélèvement des matériaux

Palette dominante de l'architecture industrielle

 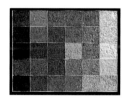 

OPPOSITE, FROM ABOVE: Many of the regional and largely rural studies made by J-P and D Lenclos were collected together and published under the title Les Couleurs de la France in 1982, including: 'Les Couleurs de Bailly-Romainvilliers'; 'Les Couleurs de Coupvray. A comparison of these studies of different regions reveals striking differences which appear even more significant when compared with similar analyses of colours characteristic of different countries, and of urban metropolitan areas within those countries, for example, Tokyo and New York

L, FROM ABOVE TO BELOW R: Lenclos' methodology applied to Tokyo: Samples are shown with their derived palettes, examples of buildings and their urban and landscape settings; Natural and manufactured materials, flakes of paint and samples of vegetation all contribute to the colours of a place; Soil can come in many rich and subtle colours; Even a single piece of stone can reveal a surprising number of colours

lected samples of paint, of stone, of pebble-dash; we looked at the colours of facades, [made] a visual breakdown, produced maps of the different colours on a regional basis and made site analyses . . . We found we had hit upon a unique method of investigation, and an appreciation of all that the geography of colour meant in the cultural world.[100]

Lenclos later made site investigations in several other countries and cities, including Japan (Tokyo), Iran, Brazil, the USA, Guatamala and many European countries.[101] Inevitably, the work extended to include growing towns and cities and new towns. The objectives broadened:

The aim was nothing more or less than to harmonise architecture with the surrounding landscape and with the inhabitants. It was no longer possible to think of architecture in isolation . . . From it one certain fact emerged: colour had an important role . . . No one can have failed to notice the new role of colour in the industrial world after having been buried for too long in the black of coal and grey of smoke and dust. Colour in industry plays many differ-

*ABOVE: The Avenue of the Americas, Greenwich Village, New York; BELOW: Colour analysis of Greenwich Village, New York*

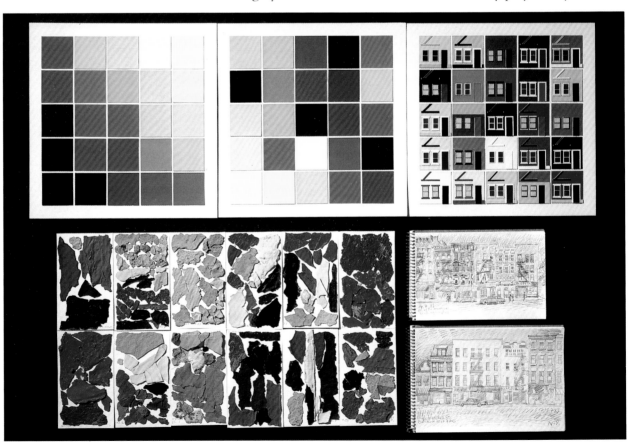

ent roles; it integrates the architecture with the site, it improves the company's image and working conditions, it provides security, gives directions, protects machines . . . [102]

The working method that Lenclos developed comprises two phases: an overall site analysis, followed by a detailed visual colour analysis of all the relevant materials. For the first phase the building or settlement is viewed from both outside and within and considered in terms of its landscape context, with reference to the effects of agriculture and the changing seasons. For this purpose, examples of all the materials that constitute the overall colour are analysed. These include manufactured material and scrapings of paint from floors, walls, roofs, doors, shutters, frames and other details; impermanent elements, such as vegetation; and samples of natural features, such as rock and soils. When it is not possible to take samples, the colours are identified by using shade cards backed up by sketches made with crayons. Photographs can be used cautiously; they are notoriously unreliable for recording colours but they are valuable as records. One difficulty in attempting to reproduce colours on a flat surface is that very few materials are monotone: a wall of weathered bricks incorporates an infinite number of colour variations. The solution to this problem is either to adopt a Pointillist technique, creating an optical mixture of colours, or to simplify visually by copying the dominant colour.

The second — studio or workshop — phase of the analysis is divided into three parts. The first consideration is the overall view of the facades and roofs seen from outside against their landscape context. To this is added an assessment of the views from inside, in which context the colours of such architectural details as doors, plinths, doors, frames, windows and shutters become important. The colour samples are then sized and arranged in proportion to the elements they represent on different facades, thus achieving an effective colour balance. The third part of the process is an assembly of the colour range of all the elements of the buildings: surface colours (walls and roofs) and colours of architectural features. Colour design cards are assembled for each facade, having been considered both in the specific terms of their relationship with those adjoining and in the general terms of the relationship between the whole and its urban or rural context; the process is supported by drawings, collages and photographs. Further research can be undertaken by analysing the chemical composition of the materials and paints and by considering the changes in use over particular periods of time.[103]

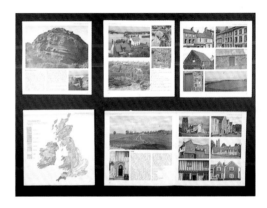

*ABOVE AND BELOW: Photographic studies of different regions of Britain were produced by the author for the book* Britain in View: Colour and the Landscape, *(Quiller Press, 1984), including 'Snowdonia and North Wales' and 'The Redlands of Devon'; Berwick and the Lothians' and 'Suffolk'*

# COLOUR CONTROL

The idea that colour should be or could be controlled is anathema to many people, who regard its use as one of the few personal freedoms remaining. Nevertheless, it is already controlled in a significant number of ways, many of which might be regarded as unseen because they have become accepted as natural aspects of our lives. These uses exist as a part of the structure of societies, determined by a variety of factors and decisions derived from nature and human nature.

Landowners still control large areas of town and country, and where individuals have relinquished control corporations have taken over. Governments have inherited or assumed the role of both in controlling national institutions, military installations and public services. Each of these uses colour in a number of different ways to express identity, to impart information, to indicate direction and orientation and in some cases to convey warnings. In principle most of these uses can be justified by their intention, but the collective effect can be, and often is, confused. There are two obvious reasons for this: the first is the sheer volume of information that is produced; the second is the difficulty of achieving effective co-ordination because design decisions are involved. There is a parallel in the practice of pinning or pasting notices on seemingly every available surface. The greater the number of notices and signs, the less likelihood there is that they will be read and clearly understood.

In the modern world environment of free markets, the confusion is deteriorating into chaos. The zoning regulations that have successfully held advertising at bay in many countries can no longer cope with the pressures of development. The result is that the protected and conserved areas — which are increasing in number — are being surrounded by areas in which industrial and commercial freedom prevails. Although these are also subject to any planning regulations that exist, the bureaucracy of planning — which is difficult enough to administer even in conservation areas — is ill suited to dealing with visual problems, particularly those relating to colour.

In this sense, the ideal situation is one in which there is complete control — as, for example, in the US National Parks. Since they are largely undeveloped it has been possible to exercise careful control over every detail, from roads and buildings to paths and litter bins, in terms of co-ordinated design and colour. Alterations and additions are required to be in colours selected from the range in a colour chart that has been designed on the basis of the local environment. In Britain, the nearest equivalent was formerly the eighteenth-century private estate; such controls probably now occur most frequently in those areas of scenic countryside protected by the government or areas set aside for defence purposes, in which the buildings have been singled out for special consideration regarding colour. This applies to some extent in Britain's National Parks because they are controlled by special regulations, but complete avoidance of visual intrusion is difficult to achieve because they are all inhabited and subject to great pressure from service facilities and commercial enterprises. This is owing not so much to intrusive buildings as to the clutter that surrounds them, which creates confusing colour messages.

*Buildings as Advertising*

A side effect of the Green movement is a new interest in regionalism. It is encouraging to note that one of the large petrol companies in France is advertising with a miniature book illustrated with samples of natural landscapes, traditional buildings and paint colours, based on Lenclos' *The Geography of Colour* (see Colour and Place).[104] Others in Britain are beginning to respond to regional differences in design, although architects are inclined to evade the question of colour.

One problematical modern trend is the tendency for buildings to become advertisements in themselves, by virtue of their form, their colour or both. The practice, which began almost as a joke in the construction of giant hamburgers, raspberries and animals, has entered a new phase of development in which the form, details and colours of the building are all based on the advertising images of the company concerned. In itself this might have been acceptable — even laudable — were it not for the fact that few buildings can now be seen in isolation, and consequently the designs and colours of those adjoining are compromised. Sir Norman Foster's elegant Renault Building in Swindon advertises itself with the Renault yellow, a colour that works well with the landscape. When it was built it was isolated; now after some twenty years it is jostled by a miscellany of other buildings, to poor effect.

Shop signs and fascias are ready vehicles for advertising, since they

75

*OPPOSITE: Commercial colour: petrol stations.
In addition to the need to advertise their identity by
means of colour, petrol station canopies have important
visual relationships with the landscape. Which are the
most sympathetic colours? In his study of English farm
buildings, AC Hardy found that, in general, some degree
of contrast was the rule and that the warmer and darker
colours tended to work best  ABOVE: The Renault
Building, Swindon. Norman Foster's elegant structure
advertises itself with the Renault yellow, a colour that
works well with the landscape. When it was built it was
isolated; now after some twenty years it is jostled by a
miscellany of other buildings, to poor effect*

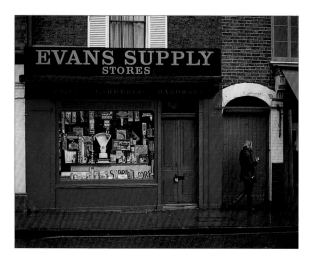

and the canopies are often paid for by the traders. This is a particular problem when they are illuminated or painted with luminescent paints because their presence reduces the relative reflective value of those adjacent, making them look dull. (The bright pink facade of a shop front facing the roundabout at the Elephant and Castle in London has made all the buildings around it appear much duller than before.) However, there are encouraging signs that in some cases care will be taken to ensure a degree of harmony; for example, on the shop front of McDonald's in Richmond-on-Thames the usually strong colour impact of the standard sign and fascia detail was reduced by careful design to harmonise with the adjoining shops in the street. As a result, the company received a local conservation award.

### The 'Territorial Imperative'

The difficulty of dealing with advertisers is that there is a conflict between commercial and environmental interests. Shops need to sell their goods. When it comes to individuals, personal sensibilities are involved and people assert the 'territorial imperative' by making their own colour choices.

This is well exemplified by a dispute in 1995-96 about the colours of doors in the conserved Georgian city of Bath, which has involved the local authority planning department, historians and designers and was reported by Oliver Bennett in the *Weekend Telegraph*[105] under the headline 'Whose door is it anyway?' Significantly, it seems to have devolved upon questions of historical accuracy rather than colour relationships, since the crucial relationship of the paint colours to that of the adjoining Bath stone is not discussed. Yet as one historian has pointed out, fashions change. Until about 1820 railings in front of houses in Bath were customarily painted in dark to mid-grey, after which green was the preferred colour. Towards the end of the nineteenth century Venetian red became fashionable for a period, but by the 1950s it had been displaced by black.[106] According to Adrian Dobson, reported in the same newspaper, certain rich people of the Georgian era painted their railings turquoise and applied gold leaf to their window frames as marks of status.

The first report was followed six months later by one in the *Observer* by Roger Tredre, headed 'Council "paint police" say white is right',[107] claiming that these 'paint police' were on the prowl in Britain's historic cities, 'taking control by stealth of the colour that home owners can paint their period houses'; this was according to a consultant on historic

*OPPOSITE, FROM ABOVE L TO R: Although probably intended to be uniform, the houses in a typical mid-nineteenth-century London brick terrace have acquired through time a certain patina, expressed by the juxtaposition of slightly different surfaces of brickwork and painted render in closely analogous colours;*
*A more self-conscious approach is expressed in the terrace of houses in Mortlake, which have been decorated according to a carefully designed colour scheme, in which the pink provides an interesting accent;*
*While the upper storey of the shops in Putney High Street is not dissimilar to the other terraces, the lower storey is dominated by eye-catching fascias, each emphasising its difference from the others, and the overall effect is garish;*
*Although sign-painting is still practised and much energy is devoted to shop fronts and fascias generally, it is rarely that they combine as creatively as in this south London optician's shop, which creates a three-dimensional effect through the use of 'advancing' and 'receding' colours;*
*The dynamic red-green expression of an ironmonger's shop front in Barnes High Street is too highly saturated to acknowledge the subtle colours of the adjoining brickwork;*
*On the other hand, an art gallery in the same street uses a green, the yellow element of which brings out the colour of the the London stock brick, while the red of the fascia has been reduced in intensity to integrate it with the whole composition*

architecture, who makes the surprising assertion that 'brilliant' white is the colour that the bureaucrats usually favour, supported by penalties of up to £20,000. Another resident, of Sydney Place, was instructed to substitute the 'invisible green' that he had used on his front door with white. His response was that the use of 'invisible green' was historically correct, the green being so-named because it was designed to blend fixtures in public parks with the trees and the shrubbery.

Even if the original colour had been green, the idea of using it to blend with the greens of nature — a common practice in Victorian and even in present-day parks — is pointless and likely to cause a disturbing sense of visual ambiguity (see In Search of Harmony). As a very general principle, the best colours for use with the greens of nature are those in the red, yellow and brown range of ochres, and black and white; yet this is an irrelevance unless the front doors are seen directly against the varied greens of vegetation rather than against the yellowish greys of Bath stone, which is not mentioned in either article. In fact, in terms of colour balance white — but not 'brilliant' white — is an appropriate colour for this purpose. Luminous or 'brilliant' colours, being highly reflective, should be avoided because they tend to make the adjoining colours look dull.

In several respects the reports reflect the confusion that commonly prevails in discussions about colour. First, they do not appear to be based on any sense of an overall colour identity for the city as a whole; second, they do not express concern over the relationships between the natural stone colour and the painted front doors; and third, they seem to be inspired by historical information and ideas of fashion, mixed with personal taste. Nevertheless, there are signs that attitudes are not totally unenlightened. The fact that a representative of the planning authority was sensitive enough to obtain an official modification of the standard yellow used for traffic markings to a paler yellow more sympathetic to the colour of Bath stone reveals that the authority does give some careful consideration to colour relationships. It is also encouraging to note that a colour policy is beginning to be developed for Bath. It is to be hoped that the guidelines will avoid such confusing names as 'bronze-green' and 'purple-brown'.[108]

The planning of Georgian cities and estates allowed scope for individual expression in such details as fanlights and porches. In more recent developments, paint has been used. In Britain, for example, it is not uncommon for pediments, porches and even drainpipes to be vertically divided to express the territorial imperative. Its importance cannot be denied, and allowances should be made in colour planning, but this should not be taken to extremes, as sometimes advocated:

> Let every human nest builder own a home-base that is unique to him or her, let each of them decorate the outside in such a way that it is highly distinctive and at odds with its neighbours. Let every building be special and different in its internal design . . . Some may argue that this will lead to chaos, to a cacophony of colour clashes, and a riot of hideous decorations. If they feel this, they would do well to study what happens in tribal and other less advanced societies. They will find, time and again, a wonderful array of colours and patterns, all applied without the aid of professional designers or decorators . . . [109]

This advice reveals a failure to recognise either the natural restraints of tribal societies or the disturbing effects of too many colours.

*ABOVE: The Royal Crescent, Bath, showing the regulation white front doors. Although there is some argument about the original colour of the front doors, the City Council has opted for white as a colour that works well with the colour of Bath stone*

*BELOW: It is common for neighbours in semi-detached and terrace houses in England to emphasise their separateness, perhaps following the precept 'an Englishman's home is his castle', exemplified by the use of contrasting colours on this terrace in Chiswick, London*

# COLOUR PLANNING

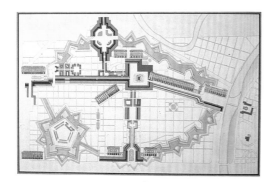

The main argument for colour planning is that colour is there already. It exists, or appears, as a fact of nature and is as much an aspect of natural materials as of paint, although this is often overlooked. Natural materials are the basis of most colour legislation. The second argument — which hinges on the first — is that legislation does not and cannot effectively control the proliferation of coloured surfaces of many kinds that are appearing in all parts of the environment. In general, these are perceived not as a threat but as necessary to modern life. We are all attracted by 'colourful' places, and there is no doubt that the first appearances of colour in the grimy streets of Magdeburg in 1921 (see Impressions and Expressions), in post-war Britain and in Moscow after the collapse of communism were as welcome as spring flowers after a long winter. But what precisely do we mean by 'colourful'? The fair, the fete, the festival, even the street market, are all colourful traditional activities that have been to a large extent supplanted by such modern equivalents as amusement parks and the busy urban centres of Piccadilly Circus and Las Vegas. These are exciting places in which quantities of colour have been compressed for maximum effect. Yet they need to be balanced, both internally and with reference to their surroundings — the places where people live and work. There must be a balance between excitement and repose, between the inevitable and perhaps desirable overloading of our senses on occasion and the familiar and stable, but equally necessary, parts of our surroundings. As Gombrich notes, 'the basic fact of aesthetic experience . . . [is] that delight lies somewhere between boredom and confusion.'[110]

*The Colour Planning of Turin*
Most large-scale examples of colour planning have been generated by the perceived need for conservation. The post-war fashion for cleaning buildings had a remarkable result in Turin. The cleaning following the *Italia '61* exhibition revealed that the celebrated yellow characteristic of the city, which had been noticed by both Nietzsche and Henry James, was part of a planned colour system.

A regional capital, route centre and prosperous trading and manufacturing city, Turin was the centre of Italian unification under Victor Emmanuel I, at which time it became the first European city to undergo colour planning. Proposals had been initiated in 1774 by the city authorities in consultation with architects, the objective being to define the processional routes into the central square (the Piazza Castello) by means of colour, with secondary sequences of colour for the streets and squares in between. A special council of builders was set up to ensure the implementation of the scheme by processing applications from owners and occupiers of the buildings. About eighty colours were selected to be used in progressions, providing related but changing colour experiences. Yellow ochres were used in combination with a carefully co-ordinated range of subsidiary colours. The council of builders lasted until 1845, but the colour image of 'giallo Torino' ('Turin yellow') persisted. When revealed by restorers in 1961, the Turin yellow varied in colour from 'caffe-latte to a faded hazlenut'.[111]

The campaign for *lessivage* (cleaning buildings by washing) was started in Paris in 1961 by André Malraux, the French Minister of Culture. There were many protests, mostly from conservators who considered that the process would weaken the stone by removing its protective surface. Nevertheless, the practice spread across Europe, transforming the smoke-blackened historical cities and restoring a natural integrity to their stone facades. The restoration of Turin was different in that it was concerned with applied colour, and so the concept of returning the buildings to their 'natural' appearance (stone) did not apply. A team was set up in 1979 under Enzo Biffi Gentili, Supervisor of Housing. It included the architect-restorer Giovanni Brino, the architects Germano Tagliasacchi and Ricardo Zanetta and the colourist Jorrit Tornqvist. Together they researched records and paint samples and prepared a computerised colour archive, which is the basis for the mid-1990s restoration rate of about a thousand buildings a year. With the distinct advantage of an historical master plan, the team evaluates requests for repainting in consultation with owners.

Turin is so far the only Italian city in which direct control has been imposed on all painting within the city boundaries. In spite of this, the number of planning applications has not diminished. There has also been a proliferation of colour plans for other cities. Among them are specific studies for Rome and a swatch of colours specially designed for Italy.[112]

From his experience of Turin, which has been the subject of much

OPPOSITE: Colour plan of Turin with the Piazza Castello in the centre

ABOVE: Detail of special textured surface or 'velatura' in Turin

argument between historians and modernists, Tagliasacchi has posed questions about whether a city can be compared with a painting (in which a single brushstroke can destroy the balance) and about how a modern city can be allowed to develop. He has concluded that to be effective a colour plan must be thought through in advance. As this is possible only for small centres, any large project should be treated rather more scientifically and conducted by an interdisciplinary team of experts, experienced not merely in restoration but in various fields.[113]

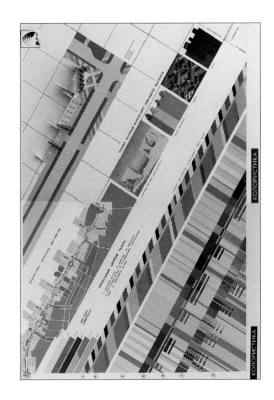

*Post-war Colour Planning*

The cleaning of buildings in post-war Europe opened people's eyes to the colours of natural materials and, in the case of Turin, to the idea of colour used as an instrument of planning. This principle has now been developed in many European countries, including Hungary and Russia, but there are difficulties where there is no overall plan and no guidelines for colour have been established. It is not surprising that these necessities are often lacking, because colour planning is a relatively recent development. Its occurrence at the beginning of the nineteenth century in Turin was exceptional, as is the current restoration. No-one would deny the advantages in improving the image of a city. That this can be achieved by the judicious use of colour is less obvious until specific success stories are considered. The city of Bruges has been transformed by means of colour during the last decades of the twentieth century. This has not merely been a question of redecoration; it is a matter of seeing the city as a whole.

There is a stronger awareness of colour in limited fields than in the general landscape. Large-scale changes in colour, such as the repainting of Hammersmith Bridge in green, are the cause of many comments, but the critics are not required to choose alternative colours. Colour planning is about establishing a colour structure within which such elements can be effectively co-ordinated.

It is probably true to state that colour — particularly the achromatic black and white — is still applied unselfconsciously in most parts of the world, even in towns and suburbs, but rapid industrialisation has generated a large number of new materials, and applications of them, for which there is no natural or traditional precedent. These occur commonly in cities, associated with shops, advertising and commercial buildings, but they are also increasingly being used for industrial sheds and tower blocks — the landmarks of the late twentieth century. Although all are in various ways subject to planning controls these rarely, if ever,

*ABOVE: Plan of Aschabad, Turkmenia (colour design: VG Elizakov, AV Efimov, M Pekarskaja) The importance of colour in planning was recognised by the planning authorities in the former USSR (now the CIS), which included a small department in Moscow staffed by architects and painters. Their achievements include the colour reconstruction of streets in Moscow (including the celebrated Arbat Street) and regional, district and street colour plans for many places in the CIS, for which they have developed sophisticated and decorative means of expression*

*OPPOSITE, FROM ABOVE L TO R: Completed colour renovation by Tagliasacchi and Zanetta for the Piazza Castello (1605; 1758); The Saluzzo di Paesana building (1715), Piazza Savoia; The Piazza Palazzo di Citta (1756; two views); Bichromatic models of different architectural examples in Turin; Avenue Vittorio Emanuele II, Gualino Building (architects: Levi Montalcini and Pagano Pogatsching, 1930)*

*The once dull grey city of Bruges (Brugge), Belgium, is now a thriving and colourful city worthy of its association with Venice. It has been transformed over the last few decades of the twentieth century by the careful selection and strict control of colour by the city authorities. The selection was based on existing colours, including the stone and brick of the historic centre, together with the small range of applied colours in paintwork and awnings. The result is a carefully balanced coloured environment*

form part of any overall colour plan. It is for this specific self-conscious process of planning that a framework needs to be established.

*A Framework for Colour Planning*

It would be convenient to base the framework for colour planning on scale, which might be considered in terms of five ascending (though not mutually exclusive) categories. The first and smallest would be the home or house, which is the responsibility of the individual. The second would be that of the locality — the street or the housing block; the third that of the larger community, district or village; the fourth that of the town or city; and the fifth that of the landscape, area or region. These are all visual and concerned with colour, and they are all interdependent. On the smallest scale of the home or house, there is a responsibility to the neighbours and the street; this is largely a matter for the individual. On the larger scales the responsibility becomes one of the community. Professional advice will be necessary at all levels.

*In the mid-1980s three villages, Stonehaugh, Kielder and Byrness were selected by the Forestry Commission for 'environmental improvements', and Simon Bell was commissioned to design colour schemes for the cottage exteriors. The village shown in the illustrations is Stonehaugh. R ABOVE: Assembly of colour templates showing possible combinations of wall colours with alternative door and window surrounds; R BELOW: Large-scale samples painted on the walls to be judged by natural light, for final agreement, before painting; L ABOVE: Coloured impression of how the village would look; L BELOW: The colour design scheme on a terrace in Stonehaugh, where it proved popular*

# COLOUR STRATEGIES

The word 'strategy' has been adopted by planners from military usage. Based on a plan, the strategy is proactive, intended to stimulate and work towards the realisation of long-term objectives. It is necessary for two reasons: first, the process of colour planning involves large numbers of people; and second, the process must be at once sufficiently prescriptive to make the objectives achievable and flexible enough to accommodate changes of use, occupation, building structure, fashion and taste. In Turin (see Colour Planning) this was originally achieved over a period of more than fifty years, but the modern restorers have been faced with the need to come to terms with buildings and colours of the twentieth century.

A colour strategy implies not only a plan but also the establishment of procedures — working methods that are both practical and economically viable. Above all, it depends upon the prediction and communication of an acceptable vision of the future. The best-known models that exist for this are that of Turin and the working methods of Jean-Philippe Lenclos (see Colour and Place): the historical and the geographical views of colour. In Turin, the inspiration was creative — an attempt on the part of the eighteenth-century architects to define the processional routes into the city in terms of colour. The second phase of restoration was historically motivated, but as it has progressed it has become increasingly clear that variations need to be incorporated to accommodate more recent developments. This has been the cause of some conflict between historians and Modernists.

As the subject of colour, particularly in the context of planning, is so little developed, case studies of several projects have been included in this chapter. The projects are: a colour conservation study of the small seaside town of Ilfracombe; a colour analysis of the large city of Norwich; and a study of some stretches of the River Thames where it passes through London. The first two are regional and provincial, having strong links with the landscape; the third combines rural, metropolitan and industrial qualities. The colour strategies illustrated are of varying depth and complexity — in some cases no more than suggestions — and all lack the complexity of the painstaking methods practised by Lenclos. This is because of the lack of long-term funding, a situation that is likely to continue, certainly in Britain. Although the projects differ, the approach has been similar in every case, based upon an ideal sequence of six stages, the first three contributing towards the plan, the last three towards implementation. They are as follows:

Stage 1: A survey of the site and surroundings, including patterns of development of landscape and buildings, materials and colours. Photographs are the basis for this stage, preferably taken at different times of day and different seasons. They are supported by sketches and samples of materials.

Stage 2: An analysis of the above, based upon existing survey criteria and information (history, geography, geology, architecture and planning etc.) derived from research and consultations. The material from this and the previous stage can be combined into a colour palette representative of the place.

Stage 3: The colour strategy plan. A range of colours for different elements — for example, roofs, wall surfaces, doors and details — is selected and presented as a series of options. Where appropriate this should be accompanied by typical patterns for application (e.g. on new buildings).

Stage 4: Presentation by public exhibition, brochures, broadcasts and television. This can sometimes be achieved with the support of paint companies, which may offer discounts to consumers.

Stage 5: Implementation procedures. These ideally take place through the agreement of local participants — which may be easy in the case of small communities, estate villages etc. — or by means of local authority regulations, as in the case of the original development in Turin.

Stage 6: Management, constituting the long-term control of the colour strategy.

2.0 THE REGIONAL CONTEXT

## INTRODUCTION

The idea of a geography of colour - the association of specific colour palettes with regions, towns and villages - is not new. Traditions based upon both natural materials and applied colours have developed and persisted in many places throughout the world. Occasionally they have been formalised, as in Turin in 1800, when a Council of Builders was set up to develop and apply a palette of some 80 colours to buildings to establish a series of "chromatic pathways" marking the processional routes leading into the city centre. The system has been recently researched and is being re-implemented under the direction of the architect, Giovanni Brino. Similar work has been undertaken by the French colourist Jean-Philippe Lenclos, who has also pioneered the investigation of traditional colour character in the different regions of France. Little work of this kind has yet been undertaken in Britain.

The aim of this study is not to impose ideas of 'good taste,' but to draw attention to the importance of colour in expressing the special character of the town and its surroundings. It will show how colour, when effectively co-ordinated, can be a vital and unifying force in the environment - as it is in our dress and domestic surroundings. Conversely, it will show how colour, when it is used indiscriminately, can be a cause of visual pollution.

## THE REGIONAL CONTEXT

The red marls and the Old Red Sandstone have coloured the soils of much of Devon and Somerset, giving rise to the name 'The Redlands'. The rocks, in many variations from purple to green, have been used traditionally for buildings, along with cob - mud mixed with chopped straw, horsehair, dung, chalk, rubble and gravel. The cob was originally left unpainted, or leached its white, cream or pink: colours which are echoed in the rocks - red sandstone, yellow greensand, white chalk, grey flint and blue and green slate, all of which find their expression in buildings.

## COLOUR IN ILFRACOMBE

Ilfracombe gives its name to the beds of silvery marine slates with layers of reddish and yellowish sandstone and limestone which have lent their colour to the area of the harbour. This is complemented by a strong black and white tradition common in seaside towns, expressed principally in tall white rendered town houses with black-painted bay windows. These are much in evidence in all central areas of the town: notably the Harbour, Broad Street, Fore Street, part of the High Street, and many of the seaward-looking terraces. Bright hues were generally limited in this context, to boat colours - predominantly light and dark blues - some of which have been used on buildings.

This tradition has been overlaid by brick traditions: the Georgian, embodied in the properly distinguished red brick Manor House by the Harbour; and the Victorian and Edwardian. The 19th century expansion is represented by a large number of houses and public buildings in buff Marland brick, frequently decorated with red and blue brick patterns. Red brick is also common in the later buildings of the High Street.

The roofs of buildings in all categories are almost exclusively of dark Welsh slate; and some of the older buildings have walls hung with silvery Delabole slate.

All of these colours work together in fairly well-defined areas to produce an effect that is generally well-balanced. But more recent developments include the use of materials and colours that can best be described as intrusive.

| Exmoor: west | 1 |  |  |
| Ilfracombe | 2 | 3 | 4 |
| Exmoor: east | 5 | 6 |  |
| Ilfracombe | 7 |  |  |

4.0 ILFRACOMBE

Typical colours: Central Ilfracombe and Fore Street

| High Street | 1 3 8 |
| Fore Street | 2 |
| Harbour area | 4 |
| Broad Street | 5 6 |
| Ilfracombe: north-west | 7 |
| St. James' Place | 9 |
| Ilfracombe:north-west | 10 |
| Fore Street | 11 |

# A Colour Strategy for Ilfracombe

In 1985 the North Devon District Council set up a joint project with the Civic Trust to regenerate the declining seaside town of Ilfracombe on the edge of Exmoor. In 1987 the author was commissioned to prepare a colour strategy for the designated conservation areas of the town — the harbour and sea front, Fore Street and the High Street — with the objective of including colour development proposals in the plan.

The colour survey was based upon visual surveys and photographs taken at different times and seasons. The first stage was the consideration of context — of colour in the surrounding area of Exmoor and in Devon more generally; the second stage was a detailed study of colour in the various parts of Ilfracombe, from which it was possible to deduce a category of 'intrusive colours'; and the final stage was the preparation of some general suggestions for suitable palettes. A computer simulation of the harbour area 'before' and 'after' colour applications was made. The various stages of the proposals were prepared for public exhibition and distributed in booklet form.

In common with many seaside towns, Ilfracombe has a black and white tradition expressed principally in tall ordered nineteenth-century town houses with black painted bay windows. This is much in evidence in all central areas of the town, notably the harbour, Fore Street and many of the seaward-looking terraces. Bright hues are generally limited to boat colours, though some of these (predominantly light and dark blues) have also been used on buildings. This tradition has been overlaid by brick traditions: the Georgian, embodied in the distinguished red-brick Manor House by the harbour, the Victorian and the Edwardian. The nineteenth-century expansion is represented by a large number of houses, shops and public buildings in buff Barnstaple brick, often decorated with bright red and blue brick details. The black and white has been supplemented by pale yellow and red. The roofs of the buildings in both categories are almost exclusively of silvery slate or dark Welsh slate, and some of the older buildings have slate-hung walls. All of these colours relate well together in a palette that is generally well balanced, but more recent developments include the use of materials and colours that can at best be described as intrusive.

Colour traditions are never static, but in the past the use of natural or semi-natural materials and the limited availability of paint colours imposed a certain restraint. Modern manufactured materials and paints, on the other hand, are beginning to have a disruptive effect. This oc-

OPPOSITE, ABOVE: The regional context of Ilfracombe. The red Devonian sandstone has coloured the soils of much of Devon. Local rock (red sandstone, yellow greensand, white chalk, grey flint and greenish slate) has traditionally been used for buildings, along with cob (mud mixed with chopped straw, horsehair, dung, chalk, rubble and gravel), which was originally often left unpainted, but more recently has been painted in black and white, cream or light red — colours echoed in the rocks

OPPOSITE, BELOW: An analysis of typical colours in central Ilfracombe and Fore Street

ABOVE: The harbour and sea front at Ilfracombe has a predominantly black and white colour scheme, enlivened by the use of blues and yellows on such details as window frames, which echo the colours of the boats

curs principally in three ways: material (and colour) changes to shop fronts and their fascias; the introduction of unfamiliar hues, such as green, purple and orange; and the use of luminous paints. The first of these is a natural expression of progress and is difficult to control (although the Civic Trust has exerted a great deal of constructive influence in various parts of the country); but the intrusion, albeit limited, of the latter two categories gives grounds for concern. The use of unfamiliar or intrusive hues can easily destroy the unity and harmony of a street or terrace because of their eye-catching quality; the buildings are targeted inappropriately — unlike, for example, the Manor House, which is properly targeted. Luminous colours work in a similar way, but in a sense more deviously. A luminous red can make a non-luminous red look dull. The presence of both types of colour is evident in the multicoloured street rising up from the High Street.

*RIGHT: This hotel in Fore Street displays the traditional black and white colour character of Ilfracombe*

*OPPOSITE, ABOVE: Material and paint colours often appear intrusive, on account either of their colour (pink, orange and green in these examples) or of their intensity (red, bottom left and right). The bright primary colours of the street (middle left) with bay windows are those of 'immigrant' newcomers from the north-east, representing a newly developing tradition*

*OPPOSITE, BELOW: Colour proposals for High Street, Ilfracombe, based on ICI colours*

## INTRUSIVE COLOURS

Colour traditions are never static. But in the past, the use of natural or semi-natural materials and the limited availability of paint colours ensured a degree of uniformity. Current affluence, freedom of choice, and availability of colours are all beginning to have a disruptive effect. This occurs principally in three ways: material [and colour] changes to shop fronts and their fascias, the introduction of unfamiliar hues such as purple and orange, and the use of luminous paints. The first of these is a natural expression of material progress and it is difficult to control [although the Civic Trust has exerted a great deal of constructive influence in many parts of the country]; but the limited intrusion of the last two categories gives grounds for optimism.

The use of unfamiliar or intrusive hues can easily destroy the unity and harmony of a street or terrace because of their eye-catching quality targetting buildings inappropriately. Luminous or Day-Glo colours work in a similar way but, in a sense, more deviously. A luminous red makes a similar non-luminous red look dull [8.7]. Nevertheless there can be a place for both, albeit separately, as can be seen in the bright multi-coloured Oxford Grove adjoining the High Street [8.4].

Fore Street    1  2  3  6

Oxford Grove   4

Ropery Road    5

Ilfracombe: north-west   7  8  9

| detail colour | wall colour | wall colour | detail colour |
|---|---|---|---|
| 2050-Y20R | 1517-Y35R | white | black |
| 3070-Y70R | existing stone | 2005-Y80R | 4040-R90B |
| 1116-Y18R | existing brick | 0504-Y21R | 4060-B |
| white | existing brick | 1220-Y82R | 6313-664Y |

The black and white character of Fore Street continues into the north-eastern part of the High Street towards the Old Market Hall before giving way to the rich variety of buildings of all periods which express the commercial vitality of the town. The latter, in a variety of colours from that of dark red brick to pale yellow stone, form the basis of an effective palette of colours which needs little alteration. The street could, however, be much more effectively unified by the application of white or white-biased colours to the windows, gutters and other details within the upper stories of the facades. Individuality will be preserved in the building facades themselves and in the fascias and shop-fronts for which a much more varied palette is proposed.

# A Colour Strategy for Norwich

In 1990 the author was commissioned to contribute to a study of colour in European cities undertaken by the Sikkens Foundation, which was eventually published as *The Colour of the City*.[118] Norwich had been chosen as a suitable centre for a number of colour restoration projects on account of its size, local importance and rich history in one of the more traditionally colourful regions of the British Isles. The city had been the subject of one of the first colour projects, undertaken by the Civic Trust in 1958, in Magdalen Street, the spirit of which had permeated later projects including the improvement of London Street (with the co-operation of the London Street Traders Association) and the Market Square. The last was the restoration of Elm Hill, which contains some of the oldest half-timbered buildings in the city.

Colour strategies can be implemented in many different situations on a variety of scales. When dealing with a city, particularly one with strong historical and regional associations, it is important to recognise both the history and the geography of colour. Over the years a particular combination of materials derived from the geology, soils and vegetation, has been assembled. To these the people have added their own colours, which combine to form something that is unique. However if traditions grow and change at too extreme a rate or alien colours are introduced by designers or commercial organisations, the local colour character can be seriously disrupted.

To be successful, a colour strategy demands attention. It is a two-way process requiring understanding and effective co-operation between all concerned, and public consultation is of great importance. For the city of Norwich it was proposed that the strategy be based upon:

1. *Geography.* Colour as an expression of the distinctive qualities of Norwich as the focus of the region of East Anglia.
2. *History.* Recognition of the significance of colour as an expression of the different historical aspects of the city.
3. *The City Today.* Recognition of the importance of colour in achieving visual coherence in the growing commercial and industrial city and its surroundings.

It was decided that the strategy would be undertaken in three phases, which might or might not be concurrent. The first would consider the city as a whole within its immediate surroundings; the second would look at distinctive areas of the city, including the central area, the Close and Norwich-over-the-Water; and the third would focus upon particular streets and areas within the context of the above, for example, Elm Hill.

*OPPOSITE, FROM ABOVE: Public house in Magdalen Street before 1959; the same pub after the Civic Trust restoration; and c1990.*

*The Magdalen Street 'experiment in civic design' carried out in Norwich in 1958-59 was a pioneering project undertaken by the Civic Trust, a charitable body, in association with Norwich City Council, relying upon 'civic co-operation, self-help and public spirit'. It was one of the first projects in Britain to incorporate a colour strategy. Magdalen Street was regarded as typical of many streets in English historic towns, being run-down and in need of rehabilitation. A range of seventeen colours was chosen from the British Standard Range (BS 2660), including a palette of six pale colours intended primarily for large surfaces and eleven stronger colours for smaller areas such as fascias, doors, windows and other detailed work. Black and white were also included. Allowance was also made for darkening or fading in urban conditions, bearing in mind that some of the colours selected were not normally recommended for outdoor use. Natural materials such as brickwork, stone and flint were not painted. Detailed advice was given for window frames, normally to be painted gloss white with plaster reveals either white or continuing the colours of the building frontage. Shop fronts were to be painted either one of the light greys or a sombre dark colour; occasionally black and white. All sixty-six properties facing the street were treated, including a number of alleys and courtyards; seventeen shop fascias were altered and thirty-eight relettered; twenty-two projecting name signs and advertisements were removed. The city authorities contributed by changing and removing signs and overhead wires, redesigning bus stops and shelters and dealing with street furniture.*

*The scheme was successful in two respects. It helped to foster civic pride, and the increased sense of spaciousness, order and unity became a model for similar schemes in all parts of Britain*

*OVERLEAF, ABOVE: King Street, Norwich, repainted using historical colours by AKZO Ltd*

*OVERLEAF, CENTRE L: Elm Hill is one of the most picturesque and most frequently illustrated streets in Norwich, formerly an important link between the quayside and the Market Place. In the late nineteenth century it was derelict and the City Corporation bought up most of the houses with a view to redeveloping the area immediately following the First World War. Fortunately, largely through the efforts of the Norwich Society — which had been formed for the purpose — they were dissuaded, and the process of restoration began. Now it is being reinforced by the application of colours that have been specially developed through research into the colours and paints available during the various historical periods. The aim of the colour restoration is to strike a balance between the demands of historical authenticity and the need to create an effective colour composition for today*

*OVERLEAF, CENTRE R: Photographic colour analysis of the Market Square, Norwich. The traders of Norwich agreed to collaborate on the up-grading of the Market Place. This, the Norman square, is the most dominant open space in Norwich, ideally situated for the display of colour because of the steep slope and its position between the City Hall and the castle. Conservation measures included the retention of certain buildings for which demolition was proposed, the painting of others and the repainting of the balcony and railings of the City Hall, but the major innovation was the introduction of the brightly striped awnings of the market stalls in random patterns of red, yellow, blue and white. This brilliant display of colour, complemented by the vitality of the daily market demands a setting of relatively neutral background colours, which is gradually being achieved*

*OVERLEAF, BELOW R: Photographic colour analysis of the Cathedral Close, Norwich*

The strategy was to be based upon a colour survey and analysis carried out in varying degrees of detail. Colour palettes derived from the colours of both natural and manufactured materials and painted surfaces were to form the basis of the study. These would include indications of intrusive colours. These palettes would be the basis for devising palettes of proposed colours for each location, which would embody a range of choices and colour combinations for each of the main vehicles for colour: roofs, walls, doors, windows, and other details. Public support, through an understanding of the principles and a sympathy with the objectives, is always of great importance in such cases. In Norwich it was to be enlisted by means of an intensive publicity campaign including television and radio broadcasts, posters and publications and public exhibitions.

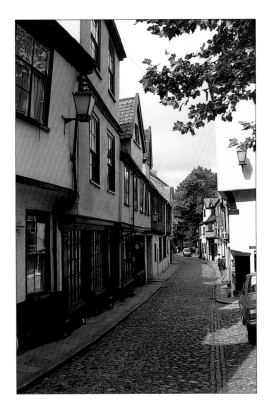

# *A Colour Strategy for the Thames*

The fact that the consideration of colour does not feature prominently in the current studies of the tidal Thames as it flows through London is a reflection of the fact that the subject is usually regarded as one of local concern, even though it is a consideration of any planning application. Also, colour is regarded as either very complicated or very personal, if not both. The result is that colour decisions are neglected, postponed, usually uncoordinated. In the case of the Thames, attitudes are to some extent determined by the quality of the land or riverscape through which the river flows. In the upper reaches of the London area it is rural and suburban; in the middle it is metropolitan and civic; and in the lower reaches it widens, becoming industrial then giving way to housing. The subject of colour, in a sense, falls between the three stools of landscape, architecture and planning. The aim of this study is to show how colour unites them.

Rivers act as spatial corridors through cities, offering long views and more or less continuous elevations of the two river banks, which in many cases have been built up as promenades. Seen in terms of movement with or against the flow, they can be defined in terms of landmarks and edges, the former moving against the latter. The traditional landmarks of castles and church towers have long since been complemented — and in many cases obscured — by breweries, warehouses and industrial buildings. To these are added office buildings, such as that by Sir Richard Rogers near Hammersmith Bridge.

Bridges themselves are also landmarks, closing the vistas of each part of the river. In addition to their historical importance, they have a unique character as vantage points between two territories and as prominent structures. Their colour should acknowledge all these factors and may arise from or refer to the historical period of their construction without necessarily duplicating the colour first used. It might have been a period when a limited range of colours was available. Expression of the structure is independent of the history. A dark colour will stress the thinness of the cables in a suspension bridge but a light colour will exaggerate them. Large areas of light colour can easily cause glare (both effects are seen in the illustrations). The elegance of the bridge depends to a large extent upon the ways in which the colours are used. Most important is the colour relationship between the bridge and the landmarks on each bank.

There is likely to be a complex relationship of colours — reds, yel-

*ABOVE AND BELOW: In Watney's Brewery (c1980) on the Thames at Mortlake specific attempts were made to provide visual targets using bright yellow for the tanks and silos, which became important river landmarks. They also have the function of distracting attention away from the large buildings at the end of the High Street, which have been painted light grey. The tanks and silos were originally intended to match, but the tanks have been painted and the silos are encased in an industrially coloured plastic with corrugations, which darken the effect (c 1980). The silhouette of the buildings is changing as a result of the building of a new bottling plant*

*ABOVE AND BELOW: The double railway bridges in Barnes looking east. The two views, taken within a few minutes of one another, show the contrast between the 'object view' and the 'illuminant view': the first with the bridge structure a dull weathered grey; the second with it yellowed by sunshine, and the whole scene beyond illuminated by the sun. The pictures show the importance of the white 'edge' of buildings extending from the classical core just beyond the bridge along the river bank*

lows, browns, greys — among London buildings, many of which can be reflected in the colours chosen for the bridge structure. The new green colour chosen for Hammersmith Bridge attaches itself visually only to the vegetation of the south side and thus gives an unbalanced impression. The previous combination of very light grey, beige, dark green and red successfully avoided this distraction.

Like bridges, tower blocks are also landmarks, but at a much higher level. As the observer moves along by the river, they move in relation to one another and to the edges of the city, being seen in perspective, then in elevation, then again in perspective. The relationship reflects the architectural rationalism of the Renaissance that is occasionally interpreted directly, as in the Georgian brick Hammersmith Terrace, which has a unified facade emphasised by white painted windows. The fashion has played a part not only in preserving the riverside unity of Hammersmith Terrace but also in influencing the spread of the classical ideal. For example, in the simple neo-Georgian red brick terraces by Chiswick Church and three adjoining riverside sites, the classical principle of unity with diversity is reflected in form and silhouette, but with an excessive use of detail and colour. By contrast, the informal classical core of white and stone-coloured houses adjoining Barnes Railway Bridge has instigated the whitening of many red-brick Edwardian houses adjoining, thus strengthening the edge effect. This can be seen in the pair of illustrations looking east under the bridge, one emphasising the bridge's local colour, the other showing how the old grey paint of the two parallel bridges can be transformed by sunlight.

The river bank varies, trees lining the edges in the upper reaches and in the central riverside parks, while other parts are lined with formal and informal terraces of buildings, which may be — as in the central area — very large-scale. In the upper and middle reaches they are often close to the edge, giving a real sense of confinement; in the lower reaches beyond Greenwich the sense of enclosure is weakened by distance and the strong landmarks become more significant. These are distinguished by scale, silhouette and colour. Power stations, silos, cranes and other industrial buildings assume great importance as landmarks seen both in isolation and consecutively in relation to one another. It is in these that colour on a grand scale comes into its own.

*BELOW, FROM L TO R: Hammersmith Bridge in c1975 — earlier colour schemes responded effectively to the colours on both banks; The bridge as it was in c1985 — this scheme used very dark and very light greens combined with red, with great subtlety; Hammersmith Bridge seen in 1995 in its new green paintwork. The most recent colour was chosen apparently because the bridge was originally painted green when completed in 1887, matched with a colour described as 'Laurel Green' and then lightened a shade. There is general unease at this choice of colour, perhaps because it approximates too closely towards nature, causing imbalance by visually tying the bridge to the green south bank. The role of fashion cannot be discounted; the bridge reflects a prevalent tendency in the repainting of bridges and buildings to use a green similar to that of Harrods, particularly when dusted with gold*

*RIGHT: The importance of this office building on Thames Wharf (architect: Sir Richard Rogers & Ptnrs) as a landmark is enhanced in summer by a unique system of electronically controlled yellow blinds — a rare example of moving colour*

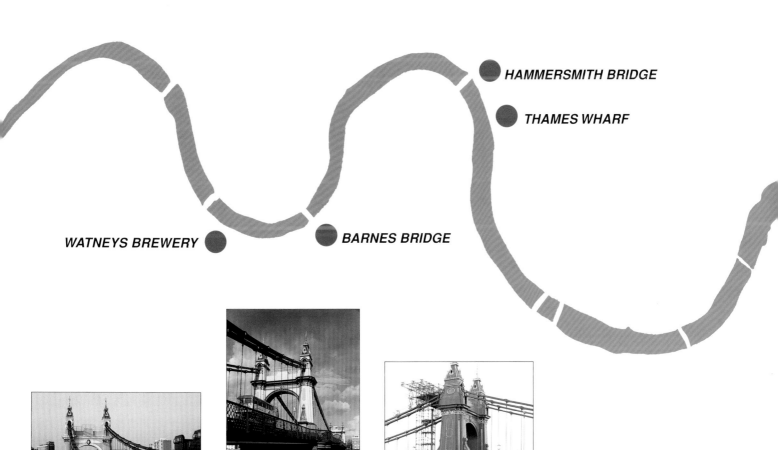

**HAMMERSMITH BRIDGE**

**THAMES WHARF**

**WATNEYS BREWERY**

**BARNES BRIDGE**

*BELOW, FROM L TO R: Lambeth Bridge (design: Georgina Livingston/GLC). The fact that Lambeth Bridge has been repainted (c1996) in similar colours to the originals suggests that the carefully co-ordinated red, brown, black and white, inspired by the structure, the surroundings and the colour of London buses, has a certain logic. Sky, water, buildings and bridges are the key elements of the river landscape. In this view the City of London is unified by a predominance of light-reflective colours, stressed by the dark grey tower blocks behind St Paul's and the grey cloud. This whiteness permeates the whole of London as well as many other cities in Britain*

**WATERLOO BRIDGE**

**LAMBETH BRIDGE**

**ALBERT BRIDGE**

*ABOVE, FROM L TO R: The Albert Bridge. The colour schemes of different periods generally complement the structure, although the inspiration for their design may be questioned (the scheme on the left has been referred to in terms of 'ice-cream colours'). The pictures show clearly the different effects of dark and light colours on the suspension stays, dark making them appear thinner and light making them thicker. The light brown and white used together on the side of the carriageway tend to combine optically and cause glare when the sun is low*

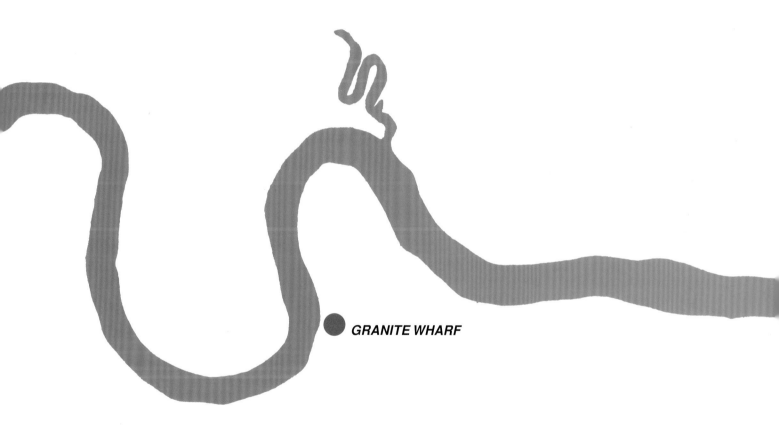

**GRANITE WHARF**

*ABOVE, FROM L TO R: Wimpey Hobbs Ltd, Greenwich riverside (colour design: Michael Lancaster) The colour scheme for the Wimpey Hobbs plant at Granite Wharf, approved by the London Borough of Greenwich, reveals both the importance of colour and the need for a co-ordinated colour policy for the Thames riverside. The clients were offered a range of seventeen main colours and ten accent colours for the Colourcoat cladding. After consideration these were reduced to four pairs of combinations that would work with the yellow house colour of the company. From these, the modified blue was accepted as being the most appropriate for the static buildings to relate to the river and the site, with bright yellow for the working parts of cranes and conveyors. These provide a strong focal point contrasted with the blue, which appears to recede into the background*

# COLOUR CHOICES

*ABOVE AND BELOW: Visual House. The small single-storey building near West India Dock on the Isle of Dogs is highly unconventional in form, appearing to be made of 'clip-on parts', but its carefully modulated and painted door and window units based upon triangular geometry give it a kind of perfection, in stark contrast to most of the buildings in the vicinity*

It is as pointless to consider colour in terms of a single favourite as it is to specify colours in terms of names. The names are misleading except for very general purposes, and the reference to a single colour distracts from the fact that colour is about relationships — the relationship of one colour to those adjacent, and of all colours to those around them, which cause them to change in our perceptions according to the process described as simultaneous contrast (see Glossary).

The first consideration must be an awareness of other buildings and the surroundings. Inevitably, these will comprise a variety of surfaces and colours, from the natural and complex to the simple and manufactured. Additions and alterations will need to take these context colours into account, with particular reference to the three 'dimensions' of colour — hue, saturation and lightness (see Glossary). Of these, the lightness or contrast probably has the greatest general significance in environmental terms, but it must be considered in conjunction with the others; all three must be considered in terms of the colour objectives; and the latter must relate to the context. It also follows that the choice of colours must be conditioned by ideas of harmony and composition (see In Search of Harmony); this is not difficult in itself but learning to see colour positively and with discernment requires practice.

The more we look at colours and their relationships, the more apparent it becomes that their appearance and our vision are natural functions that are being usurped almost accidentally by the machinery that we have set in motion for our advantage. The only way to deal with this problem is by creative planning and design. This does not, however, mean matching colours. Anyone who has attempted to match similar colours in different types of cloth will be familiar with the difficulty; but there is also the further problem of ambiguity. A common example is the tendency for farmers and park-keepers to choose green for man-made structures in the naive presumption that they will be able to match the grass and plants (see Colour Control). Nature has too many subtleties to make this possible. Moreover, a degree of contrast is natural. Our approach to these situations and to the pressing problem posed by new and exciting colours in all kinds of materials must be one of co-ordination, to ensure that an effective balance is achieved.

*Colour Design Objectives*

The question of objectives, for both design and colour in architecture, is faced directly by Rasmussen: '. . . the art of building is first and foremost concerned with form: with dividing and articulating space.'[114] This is the common view that has been expressed at least since the Renaissance, reinforcing the principle of truth to materials and the integrity of self-coloured materials in the medievalism of Ruskin and Morris, the Arts and Crafts Movement and most of the modern movements in architecture. But Rasmussen continues: 'In architecture colour is used to emphasise the character of a building, to accentuate its form and material, and to elucidate its divisions.'[115]

Colour design objectives are not usually clear-cut; they are often confused with other objectives arising from personal or commercial motives. For this reason it is convenient to consider them in terms of a scale of gradations from the maximum to the minimum visual impact — from the striking to the self-effacing. It follows that these qualities can be judged only in relation to a context, the background of the urban or rural environment, whether they have been designed to catch the eye or be lost against the background. The objectives of most designers fall in the middle of the range, with the aim of integrating the building with the surroundings. The category of buildings designed to be eye-catching includes such traditional functional structures as lighthouses and fire stations. The opposite category includes a relatively small number of buildings to which the principle of camouflage has been applied. The majority of these are buildings on which constraints have been placed by planning authorities because of their location in areas of outstanding landscape quality or political sensitivity. In the former category might also be considered a number of buildings of art-historical importance. The terrace of houses by Le Corbusier at Pessac and the Rietveld-Schröder House (see Impressions and Expressions) are strong candidates by virtue of their innovative colour composition. Although it makes little reference to the adjoining urban villas, the Rietveld-Schröder House is an important statement of colour design, which in its art echoes both nature and science — a principle expressed by Piet Mondrian:

An equal correspondence among all plastic means is necessary. Even if they differ in terms of dimension or colour [hue] they

*ABOVE: Clore Gallery, London (architects: James Stirling, Michael Wilford & Associates). The architects have been careful in their extension to the Tate Gallery to echo the materials and colours of the adjoining buildings*

*ABOVE AND CENTRE: Les Linandes, Cergy Pontoise (1976; architects: JP Viguier and JF Jodry; colour design: J-P Lenclos) Lenclos has used colour to define space, intensifying the relationship of surfaces and openings in the buildings. By deepening the colour towards the centre of the complex, he has emphasised the gap between the two groups of buildings*

*BELOW: Las Maradas School, Cergy Pontoise (architect: G Pencreach; colour design: J-P Lenclos)*

*OPPOSITE, FROM ABOVE L TO R: Château Double Housing Complex, Aix-en-Provence (1976; architects: Siame & Besson; colour design: J-P Lenclos): Different tones selected from the general palette were applied to form a rhythmic pattern, as seen in this study and the buildings in these two pictures; Selected colour combinations from the palette and their distribution on different blocks to ensure balance over the site*

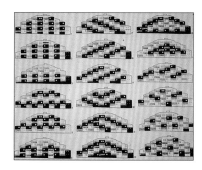

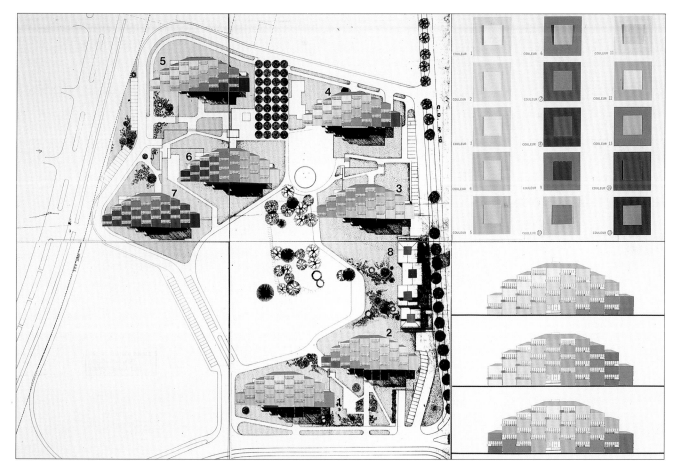

should nevertheless be equal in value [lightness]. In general, equilibrium requires large areas of non-colour and comparatively small ones of colour or mass.[116]

Le Corbusier's poetic intention is perhaps echoed in such recent examples of painted architecture as the Las Maradas Primary School at Cergy Pontoise by J-P Lenclos.

In common with architecture, colour design must be seen as an art, if only as a result of centuries of exploration in painting, but it must also be seen as a science. Art and science, architecture and taste continually shift their ground, and while the old attitudes and values remain, based as they are firmly on tradition, they have been complemented and to some extent supplanted by new ones arising from the immediacy of advertising, films, television and computer graphics. These media have given rise to their own form of architectural expression, of which Las Vegas is perhaps already a classic example. In many ways they are representative of life at the end of the twentieth century, which as Eric Hobsbawm points out marks the end of the ancient agricultural traditions and economies. They perhaps indicate the ways in which it is destined to develop,[117] but they do not bridge the gap between past and future. No amount of 'virtual reality' can deal with the concrete effects of rapid industrialisation, increased populations, new materials and techniques and their visual intrusion into the environment. Colour design can go far towards alleviating the problem. It is relatively cheap, flexible and immensely rewarding.

*ABOVE AND RIGHT: West London Waste Transfer Station, Brentford. Analagous modified yellows and reds have been used with such skill that this industrial building is one of the most distinguished overlooking the M4 on the way out of London*

# HIGH COLOUR

Considering that skyscrapers and tower blocks are the most visible structures of the twentieth century it may seem surprising that so little attention has been devoted to their colour. This was initially because the first American skyscrapers were built of self-coloured materials that required little maintenance. The colours were and are a miscellany of greys with black, punctuated by the occasional dull red when seen from the outside, to which later glass curtain walling has added reflections. Manhattan from within, Martina Düttmann tells us, is blue: 'a blue haze that hangs suspended between these sheer buildings that never tire of reflecting each other and the sky in their countless windows.'[118] Externally, the colours work well for two reasons: they are subdued and closely related, and the towers are in close proximity and compose well. In Britain, such proximity was prohibited by zoning regulations, which in most cases demanded wide spacing that produced a gap-toothed effect. The postwar southern metropolis of Croydon was an exception, looking like a mini Manhattan from a distance.

We should be grateful that it was not considered practicable to paint these high-rise buildings in bright colours when they were built, judging by the uncoordinated ways in which colour schemes for large buildings are being handled in the 1990s. The failures of twentieth-century social housing, combined with the increase in high-rise commercial building, has given a boost to the cladding industries, which now offer a wide range of colours. Unfortunately, the availability of and demand for colour as a solution to dull grey impersonal environments has not been accompanied by any significant educational programme in the application of colour to high buildings. The result is haphazard and often crude.

The original failure to 'personalise' — to give some degree of individual identity to 'units of accommodation' (which are, after all, homes) is one of the likely causes for the failure of modernism in Britain; the ubiquitous use of bare concrete is another. Surprisingly, it is still possible to find strong defenders of the integrity of concrete in such structures as London's South Bank cultural centre, the ingenious Park Hill

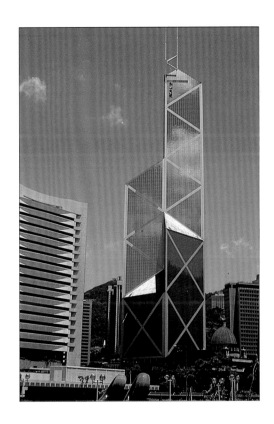

*ABOVE: Bank of China, Hong Kong (1982-89; architect : IM Pei) The architect has used a triangular geometry to solve the problems of a small awkward site and to meet the demanding structural problems of an area subject to typhoons. This at once gives his tower a distinctive clarity and an almost crystalline form, with facets that play with the light*

housing scheme in Sheffield and the new town of Le Havre. Whatever their merits, they could not be described as colourful: monotonous is a word that accurately describes them, at least in the dull winter light. It is interesting to compare them with some of their poorly designed and badly built counterparts in the East, notably in India and Hong Kong, where the residents have added their own touches of colour by decorating the balconies. In Romania, where President Ceausescu turned off the winter heating to reduce the national debt, the residents have glassed in the balconies. There are some precedents for this in the less self-conscious buildings of the past, for example, in the tall and narrow riverside buildings of Gerona.

Failure can commonly be ascribed to a lack of awareness of overall colour relationships, both within and outside the site. Where buildings have been designed in groups, such as the neo-Corbusian towers overlooking Richmond Park, near London, the problem is less acute, although a good opportunity for the subtle use of sequential colours has been lost. When the blocks are widely spaced, small areas of 'target' colour might be effectively applied to such strategic elements as balconies, recesses and cornices, working perhaps in spectral sequence between adjacent blocks. It is almost always a mistake to use highly saturated bright colours over large areas. Surface colours should generally be lighter than specific or detail colours. In terms of colour intensity, 'less is more'.

There is now a wide range of precedents for ambitious solutions, which range from the naturalistic and pictorial to the abstract and geometric. Bernard Lassus has succeeded in transforming the spaces between a series of four-storey blocks of run-down social housing in Uckange, with pictures of imaginary street facades. This is apparently a popular solution with the residents, but it effectively negates the architecture. Fabio Rieti has applied informal cloudlike patterns in green, light blues and greys to reduce the overpowering effect of the tall blocks of flats in Nanterre, and geometric patterns have been applied with great subtlety to the facade of the eight-storey block of apartments in Klarenthal near Wiesbaden. The latter is especially interesting as an example of a technique using yellow, green and greys to create illusions of recession and projection in the facade.

Such illusions of depth and movement are complemented by lighting techniques, which are beginning to move away from the 'indifferent or incoherent' civic amenity lighting that has obscured the identity of many British towns and cities.[119] Not only will lighting become much more

*ABOVE: Byker, Newcastle. By placing coloured balconies and walkways on the back south side overlooking the gardens, Ralph Erskine achieves something remarkably similar to the unselfconscious process of personalisation on a human scale found in the streets of many old towns*

focused — to save energy if for no other reason — but it will also be much more flexible. Complaints about the dullness of a tower block in Oslo have been dealt with by floodlighting that is in a sense doubly flexible. It makes every floor appear different and changes completely every day of the week, thus making it possible for onlookers to 'read' what day it is. The process of change is easily achieved with artificial light sources, which can be programmed to change the wavelengths of coloured light in (theoretically) an unlimited number of ways.

The subtler daylight effects of change on the surfaces of glass, plastics, metal and painted concrete are being explored and dramatised to achieve more colourful environments, but we must be careful to avoid the trap of assuming that quantity of colour or 'colourfulness' is a desirable objective in itself.

*ABOVE: The riverside buildings of Gerona, Spain, which embody traces of many styles and periods, show how six- to eight-storey buildings can be 'personalised' by an unselfconscious process, to express human character and scale. They have recently been the subject of renovation and recolouring*

*L: Unité d'Habitation, Marseilles (1952-55; architect: Le Corbusier) The use of primary colours applied by Le Corbusier in irregular rhythms around balconies and window recesses serves the purpose of personalising the units of accommodation as well as modifying the light and illuminating the facade*

*FROM ABOVE: Among many high-rise housing developments in Berlin using coloured cladding, the long articulated block of flats overlooking the canal at Kreuzberg Süd (architect: Johae Bernd) is one of the most imaginative. The colours selected include a dark range and a light range: the former have been used to emphasise the form and structure; the latter to give individual or local expression to the different parts, both horizontally and vertically*

*OPPOSITE FROM ABOVE L TO R: A relatively simple and effective means of applying colour was achieved in this high-rise housing block to the north of Clapham by painting one of the staircase grilles red (subsequently the entire facade was painted beige);*
*The idea of coloured reveals has been adopted for this building near Westminster Bridge — a practical and effective means of adding colour, albeit, in this case, unadventurous;*
*The neo-Corbusian blocks of flats overlooking Richmond Park rely only on the changing light for effect when seen from a distance. Colour, which has been applied tentatively to some of the blocks, would be an enhancement;*
*The rectangular form of this tower block at Kassel is effectively broken up by blues of different degrees of lightness*

# FUTURE COLOUR

The future is, in a sense, here already. The phenomenal rate of political, social, economic and, above all, technological change necessitates a pause to allow ourselves to understand the processes that are at work, so that we can plan effectively for the future. The most horrific and certainly the most tragic of themes in Eric Hobsbawm's short history of the twentieth century is man's inhumanity to man. The most significant for the environment is without doubt the end of the intimate relationship between human beings, animals and the land and sea that has developed without a break from the Neolithic era some seven or eight thousand years ago. 'The most dramatic and far-reaching social change of the second half of this century, and the one which cuts us off forever from the world of the past, is the death of the peasantry.'[120]

The end of any tradition is painful and the idea of the death of the peasantry has a ring of tragedy, but however much we try to recall, relive and reproduce the past no-one wants to be a peasant. The role of technology has been to reduce the drudgery of life and labour; the mechanisation of agriculture and the movement of the peasants to the towns was but a stage in a long slow development. The test for us is one of adaptation: whether we can learn to accept, control and integrate the new technology into our lives and environment. This process depends as much on people's attitudes and understanding as on the methods, techniques and materials that will continue to be developed to save on labour and maintenance costs, increase flexibility and facilitate change. The probable future pattern of lowland landscapes can be seen everywhere in large regular treeless pest-free monocultural fields; the future pattern of cities can be seen in the irresistible upward growth accompanied by more or less chaotic outward spread.

We shall continue to build towers, either as *folies de grandeur* to prove our political, financial and technical skills or of necessity where land is scarce. For those that are residential, perhaps we can learn the importance of colour from the unselfconscious traditions of the past or from such models as Le Corbusier's Unité d'Habitation in Marseilles. More ambitiously, and expensively, we shall be using new 'smart'

*OPPOSITE ABOVE, L AND R: The theatrical buildings of TV AM (c 1970s; architect: Terry Farrell), Camden Town, London*

*OPPOSITE BELOW, L AND R: The Neue Staatsgalerie, Stuttgart (1984; architects: James Stirling, Michael Wilford & Associates) The value and importance of the natural travertine has been acknowledged by careful limitation of the bright new pinks and purples to fine linear elements*

materials: paints and plastics and panes of glass that change colour with the light and carry projected images.

The danger of all such developments is that they will be used for their own sake, because they are new and available. With them comes a responsibility for organisation and control that is already slipping from our grasp. As cities continue to expand (Shanghai has projected population figures approaching forty million), we must be careful to strike a balance between the demands for newer, brighter, more exciting colours to express the brash noisy vitality of urban life and the use of the infinitely more subdued and subtle colours of nature.

The largely unselfconscious uses of colour that have sustained our colour traditions for so long can no longer be relied upon, even where they are appropriate. As we are slowly discovering, it is only by the self-conscious processes of design that these can effectively be supplanted. Of these processes, colour design is in the curiously ambiguous position of being at once the most appreciated and the least understood. It is the most vital and at the same time the most suitable medium to help us come to terms with a rapidly changing environment.

*Illusions: Harlequin Plaza (c1990; design: SWA Group) near Denver, Colorado*

# APPENDIX: COLOUR GUIDELINES

The complexity of our environment and the pressures for development of many different kinds emphasise the importance of colour and the way it is used. Although intuitive use should be accepted in a limited context, in the wider field it can easily lead to visual chaos. As more and more mass-produced materials and buildings appear, for example cars in ever brighter colours, we are in danger not only of permanently damaging the appearance of our beautiful towns and countryside but also of over-stimulating ourselves into a state of visual boredom.

A colour decision is made every time a new object is introduced into the environment. The weight given to that decision depends very much upon the size and nature of the project and the time and money spent on it. When such politically sensitive complexes as oil terminals and power stations are sited in areas of outstanding natural beauty, time and resources may allow for proper consideration, but colour decisions relating to large and small industrial and commercial buildings are more often than not made on the basis of the intuition or personal preference of the designer or client. Decisions of the latter type may be communicated to the planning authority by means of a perspective drawing on paper, a small patch of colour on a card or, worse, a verbal description. In the case of many farm buildings no approval is required. There are also innumerable other cases in which it would be undesirable — even if it were practicable — to impose regulations. These are the idiosyncratic decisions made by individuals and small groups in relation to the personal environment: houses, front doors, windows, gates, fences. These may give interesting variety, for colour is one of the great indulgences of our time, but planning authorities are properly concerned with maintaining a visually coherent environment. Moreover, the subject of colour is so elusive that even the majority of designers have not mastered it. Guidelines are necessary to assist in understanding the ways in which colour works in the environment so that it can be used more positively and to greater creative effect.

In order to deal effectively with the problem it is necessary firstly to understand the nature of colour and how it is perceived; secondly to devise methods of analysing the colour background against which any new development will be seen; and thirdly, to provide means of selecting and using colours appropriate to that background. The principles set out in these guidelines can be applied to any context and also at any scale, from the front door and the sign board to the industrial complex or power station. The guidelines deal only with colour, but it must not be forgotten that it is only one of several aspects, including siting, form, structure and detail, that need to be taken into account. Intended for planning authorities and applicants for planning permission, the text is set out in the form of explanatory notes and a questionnaire that can be used as a check list and should be of particular use in dealing with large and complex developments. The sections describe the principal factors to be taken into account in making colour assessments and determining colour policies. In dealing with such a wide and variable subject these guidelines cannot be comprehensive, nor can they be used directly for advice on which colour to use in a specific place, for every site has unique characteristics that must be separately studied. The aim is rather to establish a methodology that can be understood and usefully employed in the field. It must be emphasised however that no amount of methodology can be a substitute for *seeing*. The only way to study colour is through colour.

## Target and Background

When we look at any object we see it as a visual 'target' in relation to its immediate surroundings. If it is more reflective or more 'colourful' than the background it is likely to catch the eye. Buildings are seen in a similar way, as objects that are in greater or lesser contrast with their surroundings. This has been described in terms derived from Gestalt psychology as a 'figure–ground' (target/object–background) situation.

Since any object introduced into the environment becomes a visual target in relation to its context, it is necessary to consider the factors determining that relationship. This involves a detailed study of both target and background in terms of the criteria by which colour is determined. These are light, distance and surface (all of which are measurable) and the subjective perceptions of the observer.

## Light

The direction and intensity of light and the atmosphere through which it passes determine the light wavelengths falling upon and absorbed or reflected by the surfaces of different materials, and thus their colour. Direct sunlight intensifies shadows, emphasising form, but it is important to remember that the more common diffused light reduces shadows, thereby making forms appear as flat shapes that visually coalesce and seem bulkier.

## Distance

The apparent size of any object is relative to the distance from which it is seen. All objects have a scale relationship with their surroundings, which in the countryside is measured in terms of trees, hedges, walls and buildings and in towns largely against buildings. Large new buildings or structures in the countryside will generally be seen from the distance or middle distance; in the town the view is likely to be close. As the distance increases, colours become visually mixed and may finally appear disembodied from the objects. This can be exploited by applying patterns of colour to manipulate form and likewise spatial organisation.

## Surface

All surfaces, whether or not they are deliberately coloured, absorb and reflect light. Smooth and shiny surfaces reflect light more directly than rough surfaces, which diffuse it. Absorption depends upon the molecular structure of the material. Large shiny surfaces should in general be avoided in the landscape because of their eye-catching quality. This applies particularly to highly reflective glass or shiny metallic surfaces, which even when they are coloured catch the light and cause glare. At the extreme, it is an effect commonly seen in areas of glasshouses or parked cars. Totally mirror-clad buildings have the same exciting potential as water in that they reflect the sky, nearby trees and adjacent buildings, but this is to be enjoyed at close quarters — in the city, where the lightening effect is an asset. The dull mottled surfaces of galvanised electricity pylons and motorway crash barriers blend well with the landscape because their reflective surfaces are broken.

Matching similar colours on different surfaces is difficult. Corrugated materials, for example, reflect light and colour differently from plain ones; this also applies to a lesser extent to glossy and matt painted surfaces. Moreover, identical coloured surfaces will reflect different colours according to their orientation.

## Colour Characteristics

Colour has three 'dimensions', hue, light-reflective value and chroma (saturation or intensity), and they must all be considered. At a distance the light reflective value is the most critical. White, the lightest colour, should be used with restraint for this reason, as should yellow. Although there is a strong traditional precedent in the use of whitewash on farmhouses, they are usually seen in isolation. A number of white targets scattered over a limited area (as occurs with caravans) is visually disruptive. Yellow can be almost as reflective as white or nearly as dark as black, according to its value. Although it is a good landscape colour — occurring in all vegetation and the majority of natural building materials — in its pure form it needs to be handled with great care. Large bright areas should almost always be avoided and its use confined to structural colour or detail. This also applies to red, which although generally less reflective than yellow can make a strong chromatic impact on the landscape, most easily in the form of natural ochres and red-browns. Blue, by contrast, is an uncommon landscape colour and should be used exceptionally rather than habitually. It brings out the worst in grass by relating to its blue content, making it difficult to handle in colour planning terms. The characteristic of becoming perceptually brighter when the light is reduced makes blue generally an unsuitable colour to relate to vegetation. It should thus be muted or used as a structural or detail colour rather than in large bright areas. There are, however, instances in which the essential relationship may be with the sky or water, or more subtly with the prevailing light, when it can be used to brilliant effect. In general, some degree of contrast is desirable, which is one reason why green is unsuitable as a landscape colour, but the contrast should not be so strident as to inhibit all colour in the surroundings.

## Colour Assessment

In order to formulate a colour policy it is necessary to make detailed analyses of both target and background; this will be done to a greater or lesser degree according to the nature and importance of the project, but it is always essential to visit the site. Large projects in environmentally sensitive areas will demand studies made through the seasons and ideally in different weather conditions. There are several methods of recording colour information. Most people use colour photography for convenience, but the colour is variable. JP Lenclos (see Colour and Place) prefers to make sketches with coloured pencils, supplemented by samples of actual materials: rock, soils, building materials, flakes of paint and specimens of vegetation. This facilitates colour matching in the laboratory. Measurements of reflectivity can be made with a photometer, and hues and their chromas can be matched in the field by using colour swatches.

## Environmental Impact: Colour

For assessment purposes, it is useful to compile a questionnaire relating to the type of development and its context, based upon a check-list of items, which may be expanded as required to suit the project. The colours of items that may not register in the distant view will become important at close quarters.

*Questions relating to the background:*
1  What is the extent of the visual field?
2  What is the land-use and settlement pattern? Does it have an identifiable landscape character?
3  What is the predominant colour of the area? What are its constituent colours in terms of rocks, soils, vegetation, traditional and modern buildings and other structures?
4  What colour changes occur?
5  What is the quality of light? Is the atmosphere polluted, habitually damp, clear, changeable?
6  How vulnerable is the area to change? Would it be spoilt or improved by the addition of a new focus?
7  What colours could appropriately be added?

*Questions relating to the target:*
1  How large an area of the background will it cover?
2  What is the proposed scale, size, form?
3  What materials/textures/colours are proposed?
4  What are the alternatives?
5  What is the orientation? How can the elements be arranged?
6  Do the elements relate to any existing structures? If so, how can they be integrated/related?
7  What is the time-scale for completion, for extension (if any) and for the duration of its useful life?
8  How long is the expected life of the surface: materials/colours?
9  Are the colours fast or will they deteriorate, and if so will they be repainted and cleaned?
10 From where will the building development be seen? How frequently and by how many people will it be seen?
11 Should the development respond to any significant local or regional colour traditions?
12 What are the colour options?

## Visual Objectives

It is important to decide upon visual objectives at an early planning stage of the development because they will have a strong influence upon the siting, form and materials of the project. The visual objectives are likely to fall within one or more of the following categories:
1  Suppression. Should the whole or part of the building complex be concealed by burying, earth-mounding or planting? Should colours be used to reduce impact?
2  Integration. Should the whole or part of the building complex be integrated by the use of material and colours that have a particular affinity with the surroundings?
3  Distraction. Should colour be used as a target or series of targets to distract attention away from other parts of the development or surroundings?
4  Creative expression. Should colour be used as a design element to attract attention to the building as a whole?

## Colour Options

The 'local' surface colours will depend upon the exposed construction materials, on cladding materials and on applied paint. It is a mistake to try to match the colours of different materials with one another. Some degree of contrast is more effective and more easily achieved. The choice of materials will limit the choice of colours. In addition, certain colours may be immediately rejected as unsuitable:

for example, bright green in the countryside. When these eliminations have been made, a series of colour options should be drawn up, with details of the materials, manufacturers and colour references. Translated into photomontage, video montage or models these options can be used to evaluate the alternatives and find an appropriate solution. It is also useful to erect a large-scale colour panel on site.

## Colour Measurements

The viewpoints from which the colour measurements will be made must be carefully selected to ensure that they will have a valid relationship with the finished project. In urban or built-up areas they should be close; in the countryside, where the structure will be seen in a landscape setting, they will vary from a middle to a distant range. At such ranges there is the advantage that the individual textures of plants and of building materials visually coalesce, presenting what appear to be abstract areas of colour. It is however often necessary to make a supplementary assessment at close range, as in the case of signs and street furniture, which may be sited against a background of buildings or vegetation.

Three basic factors need to be measured: the lightness or reflectivity (measured as value in the Munsell system); the hue; and the saturation (chroma in the Munsell system). The first is important because it is principally on the basis of contrast that we perceive objects in the landscape. Hue and saturation are clearly important because of the need to select appropriate colours for any new development.

Colour value can be measured by a photometer or long-range light meter focused on different parts of the site. In one of the most comprehensive studies of colours in the countryside ever undertaken, AC Hardy found that landscape values in all parts of the UK (excluding Northern Ireland) ranged from Munsell value 4 to value 8 or from 12 to 56 percent. This covered most types of surface geology and bare earth resulting from agriculture but excluded such extremes as the dark sides of forests or woodlands and bare chalk faces. The value readings for traditional buildings coincided generally with those for surface geology, colour-washed buildings tending to have high values. Treating the landscape as a target–background situation, he set out to measure the background by travelling around England, Scotland and Wales making recordings at all seasons and in clear and overcast light using a pocket Munsell atlas to identify colours. These were then recorded on Agfa CT18 colour slides. As the survey

related to large buildings and their backgrounds, the countryside was viewed from a distance at which the individual textures of leaves and plants and their colours merged. The findings were described on a Munsell colour circle, identifying hues as natural or artificial. These categories cannot however be considered as precise because of the other variables of value and chroma, which are not recorded in this way. For instance, some hues that appeared at low values and chromas as natural would have appeared as artificial if they had occurred at high values and chromas. Hardy's main findings were that natural ground surface hues are concentrated in the ten Red to ten Green-yellow zones and sky and water in the ten Blue-green to ten Purple-blue zones, with a small concentration of colour centred in the five Red-purple zones, owing to the presence of heather flowers and certain weeds. The tenth of the Munsell spectrum described as 'Munsell Green' does not occur at all. This provides an illustration both of the limitations of words to describe colours and of the folly of choosing green to blend with the landscape.

Hue and chroma can be measured by direct comparison with colour chips or cards or through an epidiascope as used by Heath for New Zealand farm buildings. Hardy related these to colour slides for his investigation, but it should be noted that their colour is variable. Lenclos advocates the use of sketches with crayon, which provides matchable colour.

A relatively simple method of assessing the impact of a structure on the landscape background under particular light conditions is to make a model, or more simply a cut-out profile of the structure, and arrange it on a stand in front of the view, with or without a surrounding frame. Various models could then be coloured differently and perhaps photographed. Cairns used swatches of alternative colours to relate to photographs taken at different seasons.

Pressures are such that it is not often possible to carry out an assessment over a whole year as Hardy did, and it would be of great value if planning and other authorities were to undertake comprehensive colour surveys that could be fed into a series of computer databases. These could perhaps start with the National Parks, for which colour is already considered important, and be extended over other regions and counties, particularly those where pressure for development is greatest. Lenclos has produced detailed studies from many of the regions of France (see Colour and Place).
*(Reproduced by kind permission of Quiller Press.)*

# NOTES

1  R Osborne, *Lights and Pigments*, John Murray (London), 1980, p70
2  J Gage, *Colour and Culture*, Thames and Hudson (London), 1993, p7
3  W Grohmann, *Paul Klee*, Lund Humphries (London), 1954, pp143-44
4  EG Güse, *Die Tunisreise: Klee, Macke, Moilliet*, Verlag Gerd Hatje (Stuttgart), 1982, p144
5  A Stokes, in Gage, *Colour and Culture* (*see* note 2), p8
6  HE Hinton, *Natural Deception. Illusion in Nature and Art*, ed RL Gregory, Duckworth (London), 1973, 1980, pp97-160
8  H Rossotti, *Colour: Why the World Isn't Grey*, Penguin (Harmondsworth), 1983, p112/Osborne, *Lights and Pigments* (*see* note 1), p23
9  RL Gregory, *Eye and Brain*, Weidenfeld & Nicolson (London), 1979, pp61-63
10  O Sacks, *An Anthropologist on Mars*, Picador (London), 1995
11  CJ Trevarthen, in R Gregory, J Harris, P Heard and D Rose (eds), *The Artful Eye*, Oxford University Press (Oxford), 1995, pp187-94
12  Sacks, *An Anthropologist on Mars* (*see* note 10)
13  *See* note 11
14  Gregory, *Eye and Brain* (*see* note 9), pp174-87
15  JD Barrow, *The Artful Universe*, Clarendon Press (Oxford), 1995
16  Trevarthen, in Gregory, *The Artful Eye* (*see* note 11), pp187-94
17  Ibid., p188
18  Ibid.
19  Ibid.
20  B Berlin and P Kay, in H Varley, *Colour*, Mitchell Beazley (London), 1980, p51
21  Trevarthen, in Gregory, *The Artful Eye* (*see* note 11), pp187-94
22  D Attenborough, *Life on Earth*, BBC Books (London), 1979
23  J Bronowski, *The Ascent of Man*, BBC Books (London), 1976, 1981, p56
24  Yung Chang, *Wild Swans*, Flamingo (London), 1990
25  Gregory, *Eye and Brain* (*see* note 9), p15
26  L Bomford, Kirby, Leighton, Roy (eds), *Impressionism: Art in the Making*, National Gallery (London), 1990, p76
27  Ibid., p51
28  Osborne, *Lights and Pigments* (*see* note 1), p96
29  O Jones, *The Grammar of Ornament* (1856), Studio Editions (London), 1986
30  H Varley (ed), *Colour*, Mitchell Beazley (London),1980, pp18-19
31  Ibid., p88
32  Osborne, *Lights and Pigments* (*see* note 1), p15
33  Ibid.
34  Ibid.
35  A Clifton-Taylor, *The Pattern of English Building*, Faber & Faber (London), 1980
36  V Pasmore, 'Colour as a Function of Multi-Dimensional Space' in *Colour for Architecture*, eds Porter and Mikelliades, Studio Vista (London), 1976, p43
37  SE Rasmussen, 'Architecture Experienced as Colour Planes' in *Experiencing Architecture*, MIT (Cambridge, Massachusetts), 1931, 1959, p83
38  E Land, quoted by Osborne, *Lights and Pigments* (*see* note 1)
39  Sacks, *Anthropologist on Mars* (*see* note 7), p22
40  Ibid., p22
41  P Heron, *The Colour of Colour*, University of Texas (Austin, Texas), 1979, p13
42  JAD Ingres, quoted in Bomford, Kirby, Leighton, Roy, *Impressionism*, see note 26, p11
43  JJ Gibson, *Perception of the Visual World*, Greenwood Press (Connecticut), 1950, 1977, 1979
44  MD Vernon, *The Psychology of Perception*, Penguin (Harmondsworth), 1962, 1963, p100
45  R Arnheim, *Art and Visual Perception*, University of California (Los Angeles)/ (London), 1954, 1974, p331
46  Vernon, *The Psychology of Perception* (*see* note 44)
47  Rasmussen, *Experiencing Architecture* (*see* note 37), p93
48  RD Thouless, 'Phenomenal Regression to the Real Object', *British Journal of Psychology*, no 21/22
49  I Newton, 1669-71, published 1672/75; *Optics*, 1704, quoted in Gregory, *Eye and Brain* (*see* note 9), p15
50  JC Maxwell, *Treatise on Electricity and Magnetism*, 1873
51  N Silvestrini, *Idée Farbe*, Baumann & Stromer Verlag (Zurich), 1994
52  Rossotti, *Colour: Why the World Isn't Grey* (*see* note 8), p224
53  Although red, yellow and blue have long been regarded as the primary colours of painting, more accurate results are produced by using magenta, yellow and cyan (the secondary colours of light). These are the colours used in commercial colour printing.
54  Varley, *Colour* (*see* note 20), p10
55  The NCS has been adapted by ICI in Britain and used as a basis for a wide range of colour products. The Colour Dimensions Association draws on these.
56  Barrow, *The Artful Universe* (*see* note 15), illustration p181
57  ME Chevreul, *The Principles of Harmony and Contrast of Colours and Their Application to the Arts* (1881), English edition ed G Bell
58  HL Gloag and M Gold, *The Colour Co-ordination Handbook*, BRS/HMSO (Norwich), 1978
59  Quoted in Arnheim, *Art and Visual Perception* (*see* note 45), p349
60  Ibid., p22
61  M Bockemühl, *Turner*, Benedikt Taschenbücher (Cologne), 1993
62  Ibid., p83
63  J House, *Monet*, Phaidon (London), 1981, p20
64  Ibid.

65 H Matisse, l908, quoted in *Oxford Companion to Art*, ed H Osborne, Oxford University Press (Oxford), 1971/81
66 *Oxford Companion to Art*, ed H Osborne, Oxford University Press (Oxford), 1971, 1981
67 W-D Dube, *The Expressionists*, Thames and Hudson (London), 1972, pp7-21
68 F Whitford, *The Bauhaus*, Thames and Hudson (London), 1984
69 A Hope and M Walch (eds), *The Colour Compendium*, Van Nostrand Reinhold (New York), 1990
70 F Whitford, *The Bauhaus*, Thames and Hudson (London), 1984
71 B Taut, unpublished extract from diaries, 1904-7, quoted by Hartmann, p23, and Whyte, p20
72 M Düttmann, F Schmuck, J Uhl, *Colour in Townscape*, Architectural Press (London), 1981, pp12-13, 18-28
73 Ibid.
74 Ibid.
75 Rasmussen, *Experiencing Architecture* (*see* note 37)
76 H Read, *Education through Art*, Faber & Faber, 1958, p22
77 Arnheim, *Art and Visual Perception* (*see* note 45)
78 EH Gombrich, *The Sense of Order*, Phaidon (London), 1979, 1984, p117
79 Ibid., p129, quoting JJ Gibson
80 AC Hardy, 'Colour and Farm Buildings', *Agriculture*, Leonard Hill (November, 1970)
81 J-P and D Lenclos, *Les Couleurs de la France*, Moniteur (Paris), 1982

82 Gloag and Gold, *The Colour Co-ordination Handbook* (*see* note 58)
83 *A Colour Strategy for the Thames*
84 C Norberg-Shulz, *Existence, Space and Architecture*, Studio Vista (London), 1971, p9
85 C Norberg-Schulz, *Genius Loci: Towards a Phenomenology of Architecture*, Academy Editions (London), 1980
86 Ibid.
87 LB Alberti, *Della Pittura*
88 L Mumford, *The City in History*, Penguin (London), 1966, p418
89 E Burke, *Enquiries into the Origin of our Ideas of the Sublime and Beautiful*, 1757
90 Gombrich, *A Sense of Order* (*see* note 78), p105
91 Ibid.
92 RS Johnston, *Scholar Gardens of China*, Cambridge University Press (Cambridge), 1991, p51
93 G Cullen, *Townscape*, Architectural Press (London), 1971, p7
94 Ibid., pp8-15
95 Heron, *The Colour of Colour* (*see* note 41), p15
96 C Alexander, *Notes on the Synthesis of Form*, Oxford University Press (Oxford), 1964
97 Rasmussen, *Experiencing Architecture* (*see* note 37), p217
98 J Hutchings in *Colour in Folklore*, Folklore Society (London)
99 J-P Lenclos, *The Geography of Colour*, San'ei Shobo Publishing Company (Tokyo), 1989
100 Ibid., quoting M Ragon, J-P Lenclos

101 J-P and D Lenclos, *Les Couleurs d'Europe*, Moniteur (Paris), 1995
102 Lenclos, *Geography of Colour* (*see* note 99), quoting M Ragon, J-P Lenclos
103 Ibid.
104 Lenclos, *Geography of Colour* (*see* note 99)
105 O Bennett, in *The Weekend Telegraph*, 5 August 1995
106 Ibid.
107 R Tredre, in *The Observer*, 4 February 1996
108 Ibid.
109 D Morris, *The Human Nestbuilders*, Crown Decorative Products, 1988
110 EH Gombrich, *A Sense of Order*, Phaidon (London), 1979, 1984, p9
111 G Tagliasacchi, quoted in E Taverne and C Wagenaar, *Colour of the City*, V&K Publishing (Laren, The Netherlands), 1992
112 *Le Tinte di Roma*, Sikkens (Rome)
113 Taverne and Wagenaar, *Colour of the City* (*see* note 11)
114 Rasmussen, *Experiencing Architecture* (*see* note 37), p214
115 Ibid., p214
116 P Mondrian, *Plastic Means 2*, 1927; quoted in Düttmann, Schmuck, Uhl, *Colour in Townscape* (*see* note 72), p56
117 E Hobsbawm, *Age of Extremes: The Short Twentieth Century, 1914-1991*, Abacus (London), p17
118 M Düttmann, in Düttmann, Schmuck, Uhl, *Colour in Townscape* (*see* note 72), p130
119 *Lighten our Darkness*, Royal Fine Arts Commission/HMSO (Norwich), 1994
120 Hobsbawm, *Age of Extremes* (*see* note 118), p289

# GLOSSARY OF TERMS

**achromatic colours** Colours without hue: black, white and neutral grey.

**adaptation** The adjustment of the eye to differing light conditions. It is the process by which the pupils dilate when a person moves from a light to a dark space, when the rods in the retina become more active. Conversely, pupils diminish and the cones become more active when the change is from dim to bright light. Adaptation is an essential factor in making colour judgements under different lighting conditions.

**additive colour** The mixture of different coloured light beams reflected from a white surface. Red (orange-red), green and blue (blue-violet) lights of equal intensities added together produce white light; red and green lights produce yellow; green and blue, cyan; and blue and red, magenta.

**additive primaries** Red (orange-red), green and blue (blue-violet) light, which can be mixed in varying proportions to produce a wide range of different colours.

**after-image** The image seen when the eyes are closed or turned away after the cones of the retina have become adapted to an image of a particular colour. The after-image will be in the complementary colour of the original.

**ambiguity** The term used by Gloag and Gold to refer to the intermediate zones separating the categories of identity, similarity and contrast on the forty-step Munsell scale.

**brightness** The intensity of a light source. Brightness is sometimes confused with the term 'lightness', which refers to the reflectivity or value of surface colours. It is also used ambiguously to refer to colour saturation.

**chroma** The degree of intensity or saturation according to the Munsell system.

**colour** The effect described objectively in terms of light wavelengths, intensity and purity, or subjectively in terms of hue, brightness and saturation (for light sources) and hue, lightness and saturation (for surfaces). Hue corresponds to the dominant wavelength, lightness to its grey content and saturation to its 'colourfulness'.

**colour assimilation** A process of visual mixing, also known as 'optical mixing', which increases with distance, so that the overall colour appearance of similar small-scale units, such as bricks, is changed by the interspersed presence of differently coloured materials, such as mortar. This phenomenon was made use of by the French Impressionists, in particular in the Pointillist technique.

**colour attachment** The apparent attachment of the colour of one surface to another or of an object to its background.

**colour constancy** The process by which in our perceptions the colours of objects remain constant under widely varying conditions.

**colour solid** A three-dimensional model expressing the three main attributes of colour: hue, lightness and saturation. The vertical axis invariably represents the scale of lightness (value or greyness) from black at the bottom to white at the top, the hues being placed in spectral order around the sides in layers according to their lightness and saturation.

**colour system** An arrangement of colours according to their attributes, which makes colour sampling possible.

**complementary colours** Pairs of colours which when mixed as light beams produce white light. Traditionally blue and yellow and also red and green were considered to be complementary pairs, since neither appeared to contain any trace of the other. It is now usual to identify three pairs: blue-violet/purple and yellow; orange-red/orange and cyan; green and magenta. Each colour produces its complementary after-image.

**elementary colours** The term used in the Natural Colour System to refer to red, yellow, blue, green, black and white.

**fluorescence** A brightness additional to that reflected in the normal way, owing to the absorption of some invisible ultraviolet wavelengths from sunlight, which are emitted as additional coloured light.

**hue** The attribute by which one colour is distinguished from another.

**intensity** The brightness of a light source; colour saturation. Since it can refer to two of the three variable 'dimensions' of colour, the term is somewhat ambiguous.

**iridescence** Changing colours owing to light interference, refraction and diffraction, as in soap bubbles and butterfly wings.

**lightness** The 'greyness' of a colour compared with black and white; the degree to which a surface reflects light, described as 'value' in the Munsell system.

**local colour** The 'true colour' of an object seen by average light at fairly close range, as distinct from its appearance under various atmospheric conditions. The term is used by artists.

**luminescence** Light that does not derive directly from an incandescent source. It may be created by chemical or electrical processes, including fluorescence and phosphorescence. This effect is seen in brilliant or 'Day-glo' colours, which are becoming increasingly common in use but are outside the range of standard colour swatches, thus exacerbating the problem of integration in the environment.

**optical mixing** The process by which juxtaposed colours, for example coloured light beams or coloured patches on a spinning disc, are mixed and thus perceived to combine as a different colour.

**pigments** Compounds that are especially efficient in selectively absorbing certain light wavelengths and reflecting others, and can thus be used in the preparation of paints, dyes or inks.

**primary colours** A set of three colours from which all other colours can be derived, but no two of which will produce the third. In the 'additive' colour mixing of light, red (orange-red), green and blue (blue-violet) are primary; in 'subtractive' colour mixing, the primaries are magenta ('red'), cyan ('blue') and yellow. Green is usually added to the three pigment primaries because it is possible to produce a green without traces of either blue or yellow.

**Purkinje Shift** The change from cone to rod vision in response to a reduction in the level of illumination, which makes blues appear more intense and reds darker at twilight. The effect was described by the Czech physiologist JE Purkinje in 1825.

**reflection** The process by which light bounces off a surface, enabling it to be seen. Matt surfaces reflect diffusely, sending the light waves in all directions. Mirror-like surfaces reflect directly, returning the light waves at the same angle at which they received them. Preferential reflection causes surfaces to appear coloured.

**refraction** The bending of light rays as they pass from one translucent medium to another,

as for instance from air to water or glass. Shorter wavelengths of light are bent more than longer wavelengths, a factor that allows prisms or other suitably shaped transparent bodies to break white light into a spectrum of colours.

**saturation** The intensity and purity of a colour. The term was originally used by dyers to describe the vividness of a hue.

**scattering** The phenomenon in which light is scattered in all directions by reflection from transparent particles in a medium such as water vapour, when the wavelengths approximate to the diameter of the particles. Known as 'Tyndall's scattering' after the scientist who first described it, it occurs most commonly with the shorter wavelengths of violet and blue but also with those of green.

**secondary colours** Colours obtained by mixing two or more primary colours. For example, in painting orange is produced by mixing the subtractive primaries magenta and yellow.

**shade** A colour obtained by mixing a hue with black.

**simultaneous contrast** The effect on contrast of colours that are simultaneously present in the visual field. The phenomenon is seen in receding ranges of hills, which appear to have darker upper edges when contrasted with the lower edges of the adjoining range, or in a grey object that looks lighter against a dark background and darker against a light background. An adjacent surface may appear tinged with the complementary colour of the background.

**spectral colour** The constituent colours of sunlight and white light.

**subtractive colour** Colour produced by blocking or cancelling out a certain group of light wavelengths. Colours can be subtracted by the superimposition of a coloured filter over the light source or by the addition of dyes or pigments to a substance.

**subtractive primaries** Yellow, cyan and magenta. Paints, inks or dyes of these colours can be mixed to produce a wide range of colours. When all three are combined equally they absorb almost all the light wavelengths, producing brownish black.

**tertiary colour** In painting, colours produced by mixing two secondary colours.

**tint** A colour obtained by mixing a hue with white.

**tone** A term used loosely to describe colour modifications; used specifically by Birren to refer to the gradation from a hue towards neutral grey.

**value** The term used in the Munsell system for the lightness of a surface colour. It is roughly but not precisely synonymous with the term 'greyness' used in the BSS Colour Coordination Framework (BS 5252).

**wavelength** The distance between the peaks of adjacent waves. Waves of spectral colours are measured as follows: red, 760-647, orange, 647-585, yellow, 585-575, green, 575-491, blue, 491-424, violet, 424-380.

# BIBLIOGRAPHY

Albers, J, *Interaction of Colour*, Yale University Press (Yale), 1971

Alexander, C, *Notes on the Synthesis of Form*, Oxford University Press (Oxford), 1964

Amsterdam: *Oud en Nieuw*, Stichting Kleur Buiten (Netherlands foundation to promote the outdoor use of colour)

Arnheim, R, 'Gestalt Psychology and Artistic Form', *Aspects of Form*, ed LL Whyte, Lund Humphries (London), 1968

*Art and Visual Perception*, Faber & Faber (London), 1954/University of California (Los Angeles), 1974

Attenborough, D, *Life on Earth*, BBC Books (London), 1979

*The Living Planet*, BBC Books (London), 1990

Bacon, EN, *Design of Cities*, Thames and Hudson (London), 1967

Barrow, JD, *The Artful Universe*, Clarendon Press (Oxford), 1995

Bartram, A, *Street Name Lettering in the British Isles*, Lund Humphries (London), 1978

Bell, C and R, *City Fathers*, Cresset Press (London), 1972

Berger, J, *Ways of Seeing*, BBC Books (London), 1972

Birren, F, *Colour and Human Response*, Van Nostrand Reinhold Co (New York), 1969

*Principles of Colour*, Van Nostrand Reinhold Co (New York), 1969

Bockemühl, M, *Turner*, Benedikt Taschenbücher (Cologne), 1993

Bomford, L, *Camouflage and Colour*, Boxtree (London), 1992

Bomford, D, J Kirby, J Leighton, A Roy (eds), *Impressionism: Art in the Making*, National Gallery (London), 1990

Bronowski, J, *The Ascent of Man*, BBC Books (London), 1976, 1981

*Bruno Taut, 1880-1938*, exhibition catalogue, Akademie der Künste (Berlin), 1980

*Building Research Station: Various Digests on Colour and Buildings*, HMSO (Norwich)

Burke, E, *Enquiries into the Origin of our Ideas of the Sublime and Beautiful*, London, 1767

Cairns, WJ, and associates, *Flotta Orkney Oil Handling Terminal: Visual Impact, Appraisal and Landscape Proposals*, Occidental Oil Company (Edinburgh), 1971

Campbell, FJ, 'Current Materials', paper delivered at symposium on Colour and the Countryside (March 1982)

*Catalogue of Farm Buildings*, Design Council (London), 1977

Chevreul, ME, *The Principles of Harmony and Contrast of Colours and their Application to the Arts* (1881), ed G Bell (London)

Clark, K, *Landscape into Art*, Penguin (Harmondsworth), 1961

Clifton-Taylor, A, *The Pattern of English Building*, Faber & Faber (London), 1980

Cock, A, *Twaalf Kleurstellingen*, Stichting Kleur Buiten (Netherlands foundation to promote the outdoor use of colour)

*Colour Finishes for Farm Buildings*, Design Council (London), 1977

'Colour in Architecture', *Architectural Design*, profile no 120, 1996

'Conservation Areas', *Architect's Journal* (reprint 18 January 1967), Architectural Press (London)

Cooper, G, and D Sargent, *Planning the Town*, Phaidon (London), 1979

*Countryside Conservation Handbook*, Countryside Commission (London)

Cullen, G, *Townscape*, Architectural Press (London), 1971

Cumming, R, and T Porter, *The Colour Eye*, BBC Books (London), 1990

Darley, G, *The National Trust Book of the Farm*, National Trust/Weidenfeld & Nicolson (London), 1981

*Dazzle Painting* (exhibition catalogue), Imperial War Museum (London), 1990

*Design 'in the Countryside'*, no 287, Design Council (London), 1972

Dube, W-D, *The Expressionists*, Thames and Hudson (London), 1972

Düttmann, M, F Schmuck, J Uhl, *Color in Townscape*, Architectural Press (London), 1981

'Farbe und Architektur', *Kunstforum*, vol 57:1 (January 1983)

Ferrari, M, *Camouflage in Nature*, Prion Books (London), 1993

Fowler, P, *Farms in England*, RCHM/HMSO (Norwich), 1983

Foy, S, and Oxford Scientific Films, *The Grand Design*, JM Dent (London), 1982

Gage, J, *Colour and Culture*, Thames and Hudson (London), 1993

Gibson, JJ, *The Perception of the Visual World*, Greenwood Press (Westport, Conn.), 1950, 1974

Gibson, PJ, 'Lichen on Farm Roofs', paper delivered at symposium on Colour and the Countryside (March 1982)

Gloag, HL, 'Dimensions of Colour Appearance in Architecture', paper delivered to the Colour Group (May 1977)

Gloag, HL, *Colour in the Urban Environment*

Gloag, HL, and M Gold, *The Colour Co-ordination Handbook*, BRE/HMSO (Norwich), 1978

Goldfinger, M, *Villages in the Sun*, Rizzoli (New York), 1969, 1993

Gombrich, EH, *The Sense of Order*, Phaidon (London), 1979, 1984

Gregory, RL, *The Intelligent Eye*, Weidenfeld & Nicolson (London), 1975

*Eye and Brain*, Weidenfeld & Nicolson (London), 1979

Gregory, RL, and EH Gombrich (eds), *Illusion in Nature and Art*, Duckworth (London), 1973, 1980

Gregory, RL, J Harris, P Heard and D Rose (eds), *The Artful Eye*, Oxford University Press (Oxford), 1995

Grigson, G, *Britain Observed*, Phaidon (London), 1971, 1975

Grognardi, D, & G Tagliasacchi, *Colore in un ambiente barocco*, Umberto Allemandi & Co (Turin), 1993

Grohmann, W, *Paul Klee*, Lund Humphries (London), 1954

Guiton, S, *A World by Itself*, Hamish Hamilton (London), 1977

Güse, E-G, *Die Tunisreise: Klee, Macke, Moilliet*, Verlag Gerd Hatje (Stuttgart), 1982

Haigh, V, 'Colour and the Farmed Landscape', paper delivered at symposium on Colour and the Countryside (March 1982)

Hardy, AC, 'Colour and Farm Buildings', *Agriculture*, Leonard Hill (November, 1970)

*Colour Finishes for Static Caravans*, The Caravan Council, 1974

'Colour in the Landscape', paper presented at the MOT/BRF conference on Roads in the Landscape, 1967

Hardy, AC (ed), *Colour in Architecture*, Leonard Hill, 1967

Hatje, G (ed), *Encyclopaedia of Modern Architecture*, Thames and Hudson (London), 1965

Heath, T, *Colour for Structures in the Landscape*, Lincoln College (New Zealand), 1978

Hedgecoe, J, *The Photographer's Handbook*, Ebury Press (London), 1982

Heron, P, *The Colour of Colour*, University of Texas (Austin, Texas), 1979

Hobsbawm, E, *Age of Extremes: The Short Twentieth Century, 1914-1991*, Abacus (London)

Hogarth, W, *The Analysis of Beauty*, London, 1753

Hope, A, and M Walch, *The Colour Compendium*, Van Nostrand Reinhold Co (New York), 1990

Hoskins, WG, *English Landscape*, BBC Books (London), 1976

*One Man's England*, BBC Books (London), 1978

House, J, *Monet*, Phaidon (London), 1981

Humphries, PH, *Castles of Edward the First in Wales*, HMSO (Norwich), 1983

Itten, J, *The Art of Colour*, Van Nostrand Reinhold Co (New York), 1969

Jarman, D, *Chroma*, Vintage (London), 1995

Johnston, RS, *Scholar Gardens of China*, Cambridge University Press (Cambridge), 1991

Jones, O, *The Grammar of Ornament* (1856), Studio Editions (London), 1986

Judd, DB, *A Five-attribute System of Describing Visual Appearance*, American Society for Testing Materials, no 298, 1961

Jung, CJ, *Man and his Symbols*, Aldus Books (London), 1964

'Kleur in De Stedebouw', *De Architect* (The Hague; 15 May 1984)

Kueppers, H, *The Basic Law of Colour Theory*, Barrons, 1982

Lancaster, M, Britain in View: *Colour and the Landscape*, Quiller Press (London), 1984

'Colour for Planners', *The Planner* (London), July 1987

'Painting, Colour and the Landscape', *Landscape Design* (London), no 168 (August 1987)

'Colour and Plants', *Landscape Design* (London), no 179 (April 1989)

'Norwich: A Colourful City', in Taverne, E, and C Wagenaar (eds), *Colour of the City*, V&K Publishing (Laren, The Netherlands), 1992

*The New European Landscape*, Butterworth (Oxford), 1994

Lassus, B, *Villes-Paysages: Couleurs en Lorraine*, Batigere (France), 1989

Lenclos, J-P, *The Geography of Colour*, San'ei Shobo Publishing Company (Tokyo), 1989

Lenclos, J-P and D, *Les Couleurs de la France*, Moniteur (Paris), 1982

*Les Couleurs d'Europe*, Moniteur (Paris), 1995

Leonhardy, F, *Brücken*, Architectural Press (London), 1982

*Le Tinte di Roma*, Sikkens (Rome)

*Lighten our Darkness*, Royal Fine Arts Commission/HMSO (Norwich), 1994

Linton, H, *Colour Consulting*, Van Nostrand Reinhold Co (New York), 1990

Lowenthal, D, *The Past is a Foreign Country*, 1985

Lynch, K, *The Image of the City*, MIT (Cambridge, Massachusetts), 1965

*Site Planning*, MIT (Cambridge, Massachusetts), 1965

Maré, E de, *Colour Photography*, Penguin (Harmondsworth), 1968

Matthaei, R (ed), *Goethe's Colour Theory*, Studio Vista (London), 1971

Middleton, M, *Man Made the Town*, St Martin's Press (New York), 1987

Minnaert, M, *The Nature of Light and Colour in the Open Air*, Dover (New York), 1954

Mollon, J, 'Studies in Scarlet', *The Listener* (10 January 1985)

Muir, R, *The English Village*, Thames and Hudson (London), 1981

Mumford, D, *The City in History*, Penguin (Harmondsworth), 1966

Norberg-Schulz, C, *Existence, Space and Architecture*, Studio Vista (London), 1971

*Genius Loci: Towards a Phenomenonology of Architecture*, Academy Editions (London), 1980

Nuttgens, P, *The Landscape of Ideas*, Faber & Faber (London), 1972

*Orange Sherbet Kisses (Synaesthesia)*, BBC Books (London) 1994

Osborne, H (ed), *Oxford Companion to Art*, Oxford University Press (Oxford), 1971, 1981

Osborne, R, *Lights and Pigments*, John Murray (London), 1980

Pasmore, V, 'Colour as a Function of Multi-Dimensional Space', *Colour for Architecture*, eds Porter and Mikelliades, Studio Vista (London), 1976

Penoyre, J and J, *Houses in the Landscape*, Faber & Faber (London), 1978

Porter, T, *Colour Outside*, Architectural Press (London), 1982

Porter, T, and B Mikellides, *Colour for Architecture*, Studio Vista (London), 1976

Prak, NL, *The Visual Perception of the Built Environment*, Delft University Press (Delft), 1977, 1985

*Pride of Place*, Civic Trust (London), 1982

Prizeman, J, *Your House: The Outside View*, Quiller Press (London), 1982

*Proyecto del Plan del Color de Barcelona*, Ajuntament de Barcelona, c1991

Rapoport, A, *Human Aspects of Urban Form*, Pergamon (Oxford), 1977

Rasmussen, SE, *Experiencing Architecture*, Chapman and Hall (London), 1964/MIT (Cambridge, Massachusetts), 1959, 1993

Read, H, *Education through Art*, Faber & Faber (London), 1958

Richards, JM, and E de Maré, *The Functional Tradition*, Architectural Press (London), 1958

*Roads and the Environment*, HMSO (Norwich), 1976

Rossotti, H, *Colour: Why the World Isn't Grey*, Penguin (Harmondsworth), 1983

Rudofsky, B, *Architecture Without Architects*, Doubleday (London), 1964

'Rural Settlement and Landscape', *Architect's Journal* (1 January 1976), Architectural Press (London)

Sacks, O, *An Anthropologist on Mars*, Picador (London), 1995

Sausmarez, M de, *Basic Design: The Dynamics of Visual Form*, Studio Vista (London), 1967

Sharp, T, *The Anatomy of the Village*, Penguin (Harmondsworth), 1953

*Signs and Structures* (3 vols), AKZO Nobel

Silvestrini, N, *Idee Farbe*, Baumann & Stromer Verlag (Zurich), 1994

Sloane, P, *Colour: Basic Principles and New Directions*, Studio Vista (London)

Stokes, A, *Colour and Form*, Faber & Faber (London), 1937

Tagliasacchi, G, *Colorie e ambiente*, Sikkens (Turin), 1984

*Torino: I Colori dell'antico*, Umberto Allemandi & Co (Turin), 1993

Tagliasacchi, G, and others, *Kleur in De Architectuur*, Sikkens (Turin) c1985

Taverne, E, and C Wagenaar (eds), *Colour of the City*, V&K Publishing (Laren, The Netherlands), 1992

Theroux, A, *The Primary Colours*, Picador (London), 1994

Thouless, RD, 'Phenomenal Regression to the Real Object', *British Journal of Psychology* (London), no 21/22

Trevor-Roper, P, *The World Through Blunted Sight*, Thames and Hudson (London), 1970

Varley, H (ed), *Colour*, Mitchell Beazley (London), 1980

Vernon, MD, *The Psychology of Perception*, Penguin (Harmondsworth), 1962, 1963

Vitruvius, *The Ten Books on Architecture*, tr MH Morgan, Dover (New York), 1960

Weller, J, *History of the Farmstead*, Faber & Faber (London), 1982

'The Role of Colour in Farm Building Design', paper delivered at symposium on Colour and the Countryside (March 1982)

Whitford, F, *The Bauhaus*, Thames and Hudson (London), 1984

Yung Chang, *Wild Swans*, Flamingo (London), 1990

Zoetermeer: *Drie Kleurenwandelingen*, Stichting Kleur Buiten (Netherlands foundation to promote the outdoor use of colour)

# INDEX